# HOW TO
# HAVE SEX
# IN THE WOODS

---

Happy Camping

Love Brian + Laurel

Sept 06

Luann Colombo has written over thirty interactive science books and CD-ROMs for kids. Her goal is to put science into the hands of students. She now uses her irreverent style to put the science of sex in the woods into your hands.

**Some Titles by Luann Colombo**

*The Human Body Book and See-Through Model*
*Dead Guys and Gals of Science*
*Build Your Own Bacteria Farm*
*Make Your Own Superballs*
*Sleepover Madness*
*Enter If You Dare!*
*Gross but True Creatures*
*Gross but True Germs*
*Gross but True Foods*
*Gross but True Smells*

# HOW TO HAVE SEX IN THE WOODS

LUANN COLOMBO

 THREE RIVERS PRESS

NEW YORK

Copyright © 1999 by Luann Colombo

Published by Three Rivers Press, New York, New York. Member of the
Crown Publishing Group.

Random House, Inc. New York, Toronto, London, Sydney, Auckland
www.randomhouse.com

THREE RIVERS PRESS is a registered trademark and the Three Rivers
Press colophon is a trademark of Random House, Inc.

Published by arrangement with Luann Colombo and becker&mayer!

Printed in the United States of America

Library of Congress Cataloging-in-Publication Data
Colombo, Luann.
    How to have sex in the woods / by Luann Colombo.—1st pbk. ed.
    1. Sex—Miscellanea.   2. Camping—Miscellanea.   3. Outdoor
recreation.   I. Title.
    HQ23.C64     1999
    306.7—dc21                                        99-24834

ISBN 0-609-80402-2

10 9 8 7 6 5

For Bounce—in the woods and out of the woods.


And for my wonderful parents,
Lou and Rosemary Colombo. If
they hadn't practiced some of this
stuff somewhere, I wouldn't even exist.

# Acknowledgments

Special thanks to Dr. Eleanor D. Macklin, my "once-upon-a-time" human sexuality professor and an open-minded sex therapist, who takes sexuality very seriously and who "fine-tooth combed" this manuscript from her romantic abode near the sea in Nova Scotia.

Thanks to friends, playmates, and family who have contributed to a lifetime of laughing about, pushing the envelope with, and poking fun at the most basic of human expressions.

To my friends and colleagues at ASSET (Association of Sexuality Education and Training), who believe that the more educated young people—all people—are about sexuality, the better prepared and able they will be to respect and protect themselves and others, and to enjoy what their minds and bodies have to offer.

Ron Gregg (aka Dr. OR), president of Outdoor Research, who keeps me updated as to who in the woods is doing what and where, and with what equipment.

Alison Herschberg, my haiku-writing friend who, with her twisted humor, put sex in the woods to verse.

There isn't enough paper in this book to thank all the people I've ever spoken to or dished the dirt about sex in the woods (or anywhere else, for that matter!) with. If I've forgotten anyone, give yourself a little smile and know you have anonymously influenced this great piece of resourceful literature. Thank you to:

Bounce Vartanian
Gloria Ferguson
Wayde Ferguson
Thomas Nast (legal
    council)
Barb Francis
Karen Ramsey
David Torrey
Tom Ness
Sophia Sparks
Mitch Ryerson
Alice Turkel
Dianne Sheela Pena
Diane Koed
Jennifer Lapen
Michael Laurie
Heather Bonin
Janice Colombo
Ric Moore
Karen Salsbury
Lisa Goldy
Catherine Kendall
Linda Wright
Dave Lowrance
Linda Versage
Bob Churchil
Tim Evans, M.D.,
    Ph.D.
Maria Alfano
Robin Terricciano
Rick Terricciano
Al Dennis
Lou Berger
Dorothy Pericola
    (my grandma)
Sean Green
Linda Cowles

John Wiggins
Jan Brumfield
Dean Ahearn
Kerry Snow
Karen Barss
Andy Darling
Nancy Hall
Hilary Metzger
Alison Herschberg
Jan Herdsman
Richard Wilson
Y. Davidson
Leslie Rathbun
Frank Shoichet
    (attorney)
Mary Gosslee, D.C.
James Mershon
Tim Morse
Tom Wilmot
Eleanor D.
    Macklin, Ph.D.
Jill Suffin
Sandra Rae Free
Kenn Colombo
Gordon Ball
Claire Austin
Sue Kraftschik
    Conway
David Conway
Fran Basil
Peggy Nakis
Ed Mast
Melanie Enderle
Daniel Enderle
Jody Harris
Christy Richardson
John Ketchum

Joe Spector,
Ron Gregg, Ph.D.
    (Outdoor
    Research)
Rob Kelly
Christian Burnum
William A. Colombo
Grantma T
Bette Cornell
Jerry Ackerman
Rae Edwards
Sam Gardner
Ely Murphy
    (Cascade Design)
Brian Clark
Tracy Bell
Kerry Tasarro
Maggie Stanphil
MaryJo DeBolt
Lou Herborg
    (Professional
    Bartenders
    School of New
    England)
Pierre Mourad, Ph.D.
Joan Helmich
Beverly Brown
Phil Brown
Ed Baldwin
Betsy Wharton
Lissa Pohl
Ed Polansky
Julie Palmer
C'leen Haggerty
Winfield Hobbs,
    D.C.
Ellen Jacobs, D.C.

# Contents

# HOW TO
# HAVE SEX
# IN THE WOODS

# Introduction

You're the outdoorsy type. You enjoy backpacking, hiking, rafting, mountain climbing, fly-fishing, and sleeping under the stars. But that's not all. Like any red-blooded, die-hard camper, you also enjoy—admit it!—the opportunity to have sex in the woods. Just picture it, you and your sweetie lying on a bed of fresh moss with the sun bathing your naked entangled bodies, as the birds serenade you in beautiful harmony.

Sex in the woods, however, is not as simple as it sounds. Sure, you know the basics of what to do. But what about all the little details that should be considered, contemplated, and figured out before embarking on an al fresco rendezvous? For example, what sex essentials should be part of your first-aid kit? What kind of camping equipment provides particular comfort for two? What are the effects of the elements on condoms, spermicides, and other contraceptives? How do you find that perfect spot for your love den? What kinds of animals might be attracted to your tryst, and how can you avoid them? And how about foreplay, personal hygiene, and protection from pesky plants or adverse weather conditions while exposed?

*How to Have Sex in the Woods* is chock-full of useful, factual information, covering all the practical how-to's that every amorous camper should know but might be afraid to ask about!

My guess is you're not reading this book because you want to know how to go camping. You're interested in the comical disasters that happen to fellow horny campers and how they extracted themselves from, overcame, or gracefully lived through each specific woodland mishap. But you're more concerned about how to protect yourself from the same.

Therefore I will spare you the nitty-gritty of general outdoor survival. If you're looking for the complete details, I highly recommend joining the Mountaineers Club, enrolling in a National Outdoor Leadership School (NOLS) course, or taking a wilderness first-aid class.

I took a wilderness first-aid course through the American Red Cross. Who would have thought that learning about woodland disasters such as ugly gashes, broken bones, and how to drag a semiconscious body down a cliff could be so much fun? I also learned a lot of tips you could use in a city. For some reason the big joke of the class was the idea of "Reddi Whip in the Hefty bag." This became the class answer to all ills and the blanket remedy for everything. I wondered what you really did with that Reddi Whip. So I brought some home one night . . . well, I'll leave it at that. Try it—you'll like it!

*How to Have Sex in the Woods* is about lovers loving in the woods. The stories include both opposite- and same-sex couples. The idea of lovemaking in the woods has no prejudice to gender—it's about enjoying your sensuality and expressing your passion and desire for the person you love and are lucky enough to be with. How people express this love, lust, or luck in the great outdoors will vary tremendously from couple to couple, irrespective of the genders of the players.

## You're Writing What?

When the concept of this book came up, a vision of two overlapping circles vividly came to mind, creating a very clear Venn diagram. Two very important parts of my psyche were to converge into the culmination of my worldly experiences: "sex" and "the woods." Independently, these two phenomena have been bringing people endless pleasure since time began.

It all started back in college, where I majored in sex. I know, you're asking, "Who didn't major in sex in college?" But I actually got a degree in it. I received a double major in biology and psychology, with an emphasis in human sexuality, and I was even on the Human Sexuality Task Force in my college town. Though my goal was to become a sex therapist, my path was diverted (as paths often are), as I began teaching children's science programs at Seattle's nationally recognized Pacific Science Center. I have since written more than thirty books and CD-ROMs for kids on science and nature, which adds up to more than two million books in print. Not allowing my interest in sex (purely on an instructional basis, of course) to subside, I have continued to teach sex-related topics through Planned Parenthood and the American Cancer Society, and I remain an active member of ASSET, the Association of Sexuality Education and Training.

As far as the "in the woods" part of this book goes, my vast and varied outdoor experience includes backpacking, scuba diving, river rafting, hiking, skiing, and rock climbing. As part of my master's in science education program at Western Washington University, I completed a wilderness education block that included outdoor education, wilderness training, orienteering, gear and equipment study, wilderness first aid, and extended solo camping experiences— though I prefer to camp with a partner.

I've received a wide variety of responses to the concept of this book. For instance, when an editor's seventy-six-year-old grandmother heard I was writing on such a topic, she thought of her recently deceased husband: "Chet always wanted to do that, and I said, 'No way!'" Go, Granny, go!

I once entered a women-owned sex toys and paraphernalia shop hoping to find fodder for my research. A young
woman greeted me, dressed in a lot more black leather
than that hot summer day warranted. I told her I was writing a book on having sex in the woods and was looking for
products or gadgets from her shop that would be especially
appropriate for this particular activity and location. A puz-
zled look came to her metal-studded face, and she said,
"How would this differ from having sex anywhere else?" In
a room clad with dildos and harnesses, I decided to continue my exploration on my own.

## Kiss and Tell

And of course, I asked people for their personal experiences. Surprisingly, half the time the response I got was,
"We don't have any fun sex-in-the-woods stories." Were they
too modest to tell me? Could be. Too prudish to have ever
done that? Maybe. Can people really have never made love
out of doors? Hopefully this book will awaken or inspire
change in some of that less-than-exuberant or experimen-
tal behavior.

Other people were more than happy to share their most
intimate and sometimes-puzzling experiences with me. It is
amazing what people will tell you when they think their
story will be in print. I don't know if it's pride or not wanting to be thought of as boring, but when you look official,
with notebook in hand, would-be storytellers spew out some
fascinating stuff.

## Warning!

Having sex in the woods can be a high-risk endeavor,
depending on with whom, how, and where you choose to

have it, and your chosen contraceptive or safer-sex device. While every effort has been made to ensure that this book reflects current practices, sex-in-the-woods techniques, procedures, rules, and mores change constantly. This book is intended as a guide and is not to replace your good judgment, values, and level of comfort. Happy exploring!

# Chapter 1

## PACKING FOR SEX AND OTHER EMERGENCIES

*Mountain vacation.*
*Loved one hiking by my side.*
*Condoms in my pack.*
—ALISON HERSCHBERG

**E**xpect the unexpected" has been a prevalent theme since the first graffiti was etched onto a cave wall. The Boy Scouts' motto "Be prepared" is drilled into every prepubescent scout's head. In order to avoid outdoor disaster, the Mountaineers have a list of "The Ten Essentials of Mountaineering." They are:

- Map of area
- Compass
- Flashlight (along with extra bulb and batteries)
- Extra food
- Extra clothing (socks, mitts, sweaters, long johns, scarf)
- Sunglasses
- Pocket knife
- Matches in a waterproof container
- Candle or fire-starter
- First-aid kit

Anytime you're out in the woods, it's important to keep the Mountaineers in mind. Take along their ten essentials. But when sex is on your horizon, there are some essentials the Mountaineers wouldn't think about. Being prepared for unexpected sex increases the possibilities for success. To make sure you're ready for anything, there are a few key things you might want to consider as you begin packing your gear.

## The "Safe" First-Aid Kit

In all the first-aid kits I've seen and all the wilderness first-aid courses I've taken, not once was there inclusion or mention of birth control or safer-sex devices. First-aid kits have treatments for everything from deep gashes and broken bones to abscesses and snakebites, but none deal with the inevitable possibility of lovemaking. Courses discuss the need to carry a big sanitary napkin to sop up oozing blood from knife wounds and other woodland mishaps, but that's as close as they come to any personal reproductive hygiene.

Graffiti seen on an outhouse wall:

---

*"Women unite—*
*Let him sleep in*
*the wet spot tonight!"*

---

### Condoms

If you could bring only one sex-related product, hands down (or is that "hands on"?), it should be condoms. Condoms have the obvious advantage of preventing unwanted pregnancy and exposure to diseases. But their special contribution on a camping trip is helping you avoid the mess factor. Even if you don't normally use them at home, keep in mind that condoms keep that whole goopy excretion contained. This means the female camper doesn't have to deal with any "inconvenience" as she's hiking the next day. It also means there's less of a wet spot to contend with in the confines of a sleeping bag. And condoms have the additional advantages of ease of disposal and elimination of some of those tempting sex smells that might attract certain creatures that go bump in the night.

To be more effective as birth control, condoms should be used in conjunction with a spermicide: a contraceptive jelly or foam. The combination provides both a physical and chemical sperm barrier. This is particularly helpful if the condom breaks. Unfortunately, jelly and foam make a slimy mess that is particularly hard to contend with in the out-of-doors.

---

### FIRST-AID SEX-KIT CONTENTS

- Condoms
  (regular and
  lubricated)
- Contraception
- Baby wipes
- Kleenex
- Lubricant
- Insect repellant
  (DEET-free)
- Sunglasses
- Benadryl
- Band-Aids

- Towel
- Rubber gloves
- Breath mints
- Saran wrap
- Ziploc bags
- Foille ointment
  (for burns)
- Aloe vera gel
  (for burns)
- Carmex lip balm
- Monistat
- Washcloth

---

**Contraceptive Options**

The special challenges of sex in the woods make some contraceptive options better than others. Here are a few to consider.

**Spermicide film.** The spermicide manufacturers have come to our rescue and created a vaginal contraceptive film, VCF. Likely to become every randy camper's new best friend, spermicide film is a two-inch-square patch of dehydrated spermicide. When sex is imminent, but before the breathing in the tent gets louder than a freight train, the film is called to action. It gets folded up with very dry hands, stuffed up the vagina, and left near the cervix to rehydrate and take its position to kill off wayward sperm. The very-dry-hands part is important, since the spermicide is activated by moisture.

VCF, made by Apothecus Pharmaceutal Corp., is available at most pharmacies and grocery stores, and this stuff has many advantages for campers. It's cheap, it's not messy, and it contains Nonoxynol 9, which not only kills sperm but helps protect against sexually transmitted diseases. It's ready fifteen minutes after insertion, it's good for a whole hour, it's practically weightless, and it's no bigger than a credit card. (See the Resources section at the end of the book.)

**Contraceptive gel.** If spermicide film is unavailable, look for a relatively new contraceptive gel called Advantage 24. It's a bioadhesive gel that comes in a prefilled applicator, so you don't have to use precious space to pack a gel tube and separate applicators. To use it, you pop the top off the applicator and insert it into the vagina. The gel is good for one ejaculate and is effective for up to twenty-four hours. So if you're more prolific than that, or hope to be, bring spares. Although this tampon-sized device takes up a little more space than the film, in the grand scheme of the backpack, it's negligible.

**Sponge.** The contraceptive sponge is not the ideal method for campers. Though it's now off the market, many people (like Elaine on *Seinfeld*) have extras stockpiled. So if you're a sponge fanatic and the event is "sponge worthy," bring it along. Keep in mind that, though lightweight, sponges are bulky in comparison with other choices. Also, since they require immersion in water, you'll need to either douse it in Evian or sterilize water at your campsite—a hassle in the heat of the moment. (A hassle anytime!) You'll also need to dispose of a big postcoital mess.

*Emergency contraception.* Another item for your first-aid kit is the Emergency Contraceptive Pill (ECP). This method even passes muster with the FDA. Emergency contraception is basically a short, strong blast of hormones via an extra high dose of regular birth-control pills. To prevent pregnancy, they are taken within three days of "untimely ejaculation." (As the name implies, emergency contraception is not a replacement for your regular birth-control method. It is recommended only for situations such as "Oh, #*@*#, the condom broke," or when the smell of the campfire overtakes one's common sense.)

So don't forget to take along a pack of these special birth-control pills, as well as some antinausea medication. The pills might make you queasy, but a little nausea on your trip sure beats a surprise pregnancy. These pills are a new must for most sex first-aid kits if the female partner is not on the pill already. So remember to get them from your doctor or pharmacist before you go. For more information, call toll free 1-888-(NOT-2-LATE). (Note: Emergency contraception pills are not to be confused with the RU-486 "abortion pill," or the aspirin-between-the-knees birth-control method that your mother might have suggested. These pills will not stop a pregnancy if a female is already pregnant.)

*Preven.* In 1998 the FDA approved the first specially designed emergency contraception kit, called Preven. The kit contains four high-dosage estrogen and progestin birth-control pills, a pregnancy test, and a detailed patient-information booklet. Women are directed to take two pills within seventy-two hours after unprotected sex, plus two more twelve hours later—a regimen that is expected to achieve a 75 percent success rate. The hormones interfere with the implantation of a fertilized egg. So if by chance an egg has been fertilized, it won't be able to settle in for its nine-month development—it will just pass on through. In some states Preven is available over the counter. Ask your pharmacist. (See Resources.)

Warning! Read the labels on all of these contraceptive products thoroughly before using them. If you have any questions, consult a physician.

## Lubricant Review

Lubricants reduce the friction level during lovemaking, especially if the partners do not produce enough lubricants of their own. When purchasing lubricants, there are a few things you might want to consider. The first is stringiness. It's no fun, after applying a lubricant to your body, to have a string of product trailing along as you put the bottle down. The next thing to consider is odor. It is entirely probable that your nose will be near this stuff, so consider whether you'll be attracted or distracted by the smell. You'll also want to make sure the size of the lube container is convenient for your purposes. (No glass containers.) And last but certainly not least is the flavor of the gel. If the straight taste doesn't appeal to you, consider one of the flavored gels that are available.

Several brands are on the market, and the following have been assessed for their longevity and stringiness. Experiment!

- *Aqua*. Excellent. Stays wet and is not stringy. I first discovered it in a little San Francisco drugstore. It might be hard to find, but a treasure if you find it.

- **Wet**. Stringy, but readily available.
- **K-Y Liquid**. Great. It's available in most drug-stores, but it's a little pricey (five dollars for two ounces). Not stringy, doesn't get sticky, and doesn't dry up.
- **AstroGlide**. A little stringy but stays slippery for a long time.

## Hot and Cold Sex

Weather conditions play a part in any outdoor sport, including sex. It is unknown whether diaphragm cream loses its spermicidal effectiveness when it's frozen, but a log of frozen cream could chill even the most rugged woman's lustful desires in a real hurry.

And frozen condoms—well, those aren't going to work very well. A condom that gets frozen solid could crack, rendering it pretty much useless. When I put a few in my freezer to test what would happen, the frozen condoms thawed pretty quickly once the frozen lubricant was chiseled off. But the structural integrity of the latex took quite a hit. It didn't take much prodding with my finger to rip the things to shrapnel. Imagine the ease in which some big guy's appendage could do the same. Just say no to frozen condoms!

Don't carry condoms where they might get overheated and melt. Don't keep them in your pocket as you paddle!

Once you've gathered all your sex stuff together, you might want to keep it all in an insulated container. If you're going to be out in extreme weather—whether it's extremely hot (over 100 degrees) or extremely cold (below freezing)—take heed as to how you pack your spermicide creams and gels and other sex-related liquids. Several companies—Outdoor Research, Eddie Bauer, and Arctic Zone, to name a few—make small thermal coolers and containers. (In a real pinch, you could stop at Wal-Mart and pick up a thermal lunch bag.)

# The Proper Sleeping Equipment

Equipment can make or break a camping trip. When Ingrid and her new husband were planning a backpacking honeymoon, it sounded romantic to this active Pacific Northwest couple. Since neither was a superexperienced backpacker, they borrowed gear for the expedition. Cliff assured Ingrid that he would "take care of the honeymoon." She wondered what that meant, but she didn't dare question him on his mission.

Take care of it he did. Not being the most conscientious preplanner, he never checked the borrowed gear before they set out on their trek. So that first evening, as Ingrid was blissfully putting up the tent, she heard off in the distance, "Oh, shit!" In her sweetest newlywed voice, she replied, "What's the matter, darling?"

Wouldn't you know it—the sleeping bags Cliff had borrowed were mummy bags. And to add to their inappropriateness, they didn't unzip!

Newlyweds that they were, Cliff and Ingrid did manage to make mad passionate love into the wee hours of the night—in the wee space of one mummy bag. They rolled over and over simultaneously (of course) as they cozily slept all night long—in one bag.

There are several ways to avoid such mishaps when it's your turn to make love in the woods. First, learn what you need to know about possible sleeping gear.

## Mating Sleeping Bags

You've probably heard rumors that two separate sleeping bags can be zipped together. But when you and a pal attempt to test this technological phenomenon, they seldom match. Unless you are very lucky, it's safer to buy two of the same brand of sleeping bags and to buy them at the same time. This way you can work out all the bugs in the store instead of at your campsite, like our honeymooners Cliff and Ingrid.

When buying mating sleeping bags, make sure you get a left-entry one and a right-entry one. That means when you lie down flat in the bags, one of you will have the zipper on your left and one will have the zipper on the right. This gives you the longer flap on the ground for your head and pillow. We could start a camping standard—men buy left-entry bags and women buy right-entry bags!

Several companies make these bags. Check out the mummy bags made by Sierra Design. Two of them zip together easily, and the opening goes down far enough to create a large butterfly-shaped space for two. The zipper will be down the front and up the back of your little love nest. You both might need to stick your feet in the bottom of one bag for a while, but there's plenty of room for recreation and then for sleeping.

### Therm-a-Coupl'R 25

Another way to defeat the solo-sleeping-bag dilemma is the Therm-a-Coupl'R 25, by Cascade Designs. (Caribou Company carries a similar product, called the Couple Kit.) Therm-a-Coupl'R 25 essentially joins two single wide sleeping pads. It is the width of an opened-up rectangular sleeping bag, which allows room for two to lie down side by side. For your top layer of warmth, you zip one sleeping bag all the way around, leaving an opening at the top for your heads. Therm-a-Coupl'R 25 goes on the bottom of the happy couple and has two large pockets, one for each of your Therm-a-Rests or mattresses. With your Therm-a-Rests tucked safely inside your Coupler, they can't slide apart or slip up or down—what a convenience! (See Resources.)

In addition to the advantage of allowing two people to sleep together in entangled postlovemaking slumber, the Therm-a-Coupl'R 25 requires only one sleeping bag, so only one person has the burden of carrying it. This helps answer the age-old chivalry question of whether the man should carry the woman's sleeping bag.

If you have ever tried to sleep next to someone while you're both on unattached sleep pads, you can see the pleasant solution that Therm-a-Coupl'R 25 provides. Even one person has a hard time keeping a ripstop nylon sleeping bag on a nylon sleep pad—it's like trying to hold on to a greased pig.

### Staytek Double Wide Therm-a-Rest

Another way around the slip-slide problem is a Staytek Double Wide Therm-a-Rest inflatable pad, also by Cascade Designs. This fifty-three-inch-wide pad requires no special instructions, has no special pockets, and doesn't need to fit together with any zippered equipment. Its low-slip surface keeps you in place, and it's wide enough for two sleeping or lovemaking bodies. No wonder their slogan is "Therm-a-Rest—Sleep with the best!"

Again, make sure your sleeping bag and the item you choose have compatible zippers and that everything fits together before the purchase. A dark tent is no place for unpleasant surprises.

## Undergarments: Function or Fashion?

Now that we've got the sleeping gear covered, what are you going to wear while you sleep? When Patagonia comes out with crotchless underwear, the question will be answered definitively. Until then I will continue to waver as I pack for outdoor excursions. Should I bring comfortable, sweat-resistant bottom protectors? Or scant, lacy wedgie inducers? What's a healthy, seductive woman to do? I've juggled my research between Victoria's Secret and outdoor-equipment stores, and as you might guess, there isn't much overlap. Victoria's Secret's supersexy garments aren't particularly designed for the rugged outdoor woman—not that the thongs and the Second Skin satin bras weigh much or take up that much space in a backpack (or on your body, for that matter).

It's hard to feel sexy when you're uncomfortable. Packing for an erotic outdoor adventure requires a bit of practicality. Some sensible items do combine the best of comfort with sensuality.

## Women's Outdoor Clothing Systems

Zanika Sportswear saves the day. They make great woman's sportswear with what they refer to as the "female fly." Yes, it really splits open on the spot. Just pull it open—no zipper, no pulling down. Oh, the possibilities are endless! This is how they describe it in their catalog:

> *Zanika Sportswear offers Fit and Function unheard of for women. Zanika features a unique "female fly" allowing women to answer "nature's call without removing it all." Invisible zippers and pull-apart layers are employed in each discreet garment from our underwear to our outerwear.*

Couldn't have said it better myself! "Nature" calls several times a day. To be able just to squat without fanfare and risk of exposure to the elements makes this a very handy and wonderful feature. And for our particular purpose, it's a godsend. Have you ever been hiking along when nature of another kind took over, but you weren't in a place where lying down for an all-out three-hour romp was appropriate? Well, here's the answer! The opening is just right for that impromptu encounter.

The Women's Outdoor Clothing System has everything from skivvies and Long Jaynes Thermalwear (cute, huh?) to shorts and wind pants. They have a long line of stuff featuring the famous "Zanika advantage."

**Wild Roses**

Outdoor Research's (OR) new line of women's clothing—Wild Roses (of Switzerland)—is a women's technical outdoor clothing line. It features the P-System, which has a zipper system from below the waist to below the crotch. Outer zippers and foldaway inner layers all line up so that, from pile pants to underwear, they can be opened up and you don't have to take all your clothes off. If you're in the backcountry in winter and get the hots in the snow, you're in luck, since P-System clothing opens up (as described in the catalog) "for extra ventilation and easy entry." Simply flop down in the snow and unzip your Wild Roses clothing.

**Moving Comfort**

If you're worried about sweating and putting on the same stinky skivvies or bra the next day, Moving Comfort has come to your rescue. They make bras and camisoles out of a fabric called QuickWick, which does just what the name implies. And they don't hold the stink, as those old polypropylene undergarments used to. Moving Comfort also makes undies called Quick-Dry Travel Briefs in a polyester-spandex blend that keeps you dry all day, thus eliminating the chafing that leads to a rash, which then leads to "Not tonight, honey, my bottom is raw." You can even rinse them out and they'll dry overnight—yet another good use for that clothesline you've erected to hang your candle lantern (see Chapter 4). The Moving Comfort line is available through TravelSmith, REI, and other sport outlets.

## Struggle-Free, Zip-Front Bra

The name says it all. Title Nine Sports has been catering to active women for years, and this product definitely has the active woman in mind. Sometimes easy access to your breasts is just necessary. For these occasions the Struggle-Free, Zip-Front Bra is just what the doctor ordered. It has molded cups, so it won't squish you flat. The zipper is cloth-backed, so it won't show teeth marks. The bra is available in white or black.

## X-rated Undies

Now, if you're looking for the kinkier stuff, there's always Frederick's of Hollywood, with its long line of crotchless, zipless, topless, and bottomless lingerie.

And if you're really pushing the envelope, you can get on the mailing list of an establishment like Voyages. They religiously send out XXX-rated catalogs full of clothing, videos, toys, tools, and books. Like so many other explicit sex-gear providers, Voyages has a catalog so detailed that just browsing through it can spur the dullest of imaginations. It adds a new dimension to "let your fingers do the walking."

I registered to get on Voyages's mailing list under a slightly different spelling of my own name. The misspelled name serves as a visual screening technique: When a catalog comes in the mail, I can decide who gets to be present when I open it.

By cybersnooping, I came up with a few other places where you might like to go shopping before setting out on your outdoor adventure. For the websites, see Resources.

- *A Nice Place to Buy Lingerie.* Their items make Victoria's Secret look like Fruit of the Loom.
- *The Sex Mall's Sextoy Warehouse.* This is the mother lode of steamy shopping places. It links you to a plethora of sex stuff in all shapes, sizes, colors, and styles. Some of the web pages can't be found (they're probably short-circuited), but for the most part, if you need it, you can buy it here.
- *Wicked Temptations.* They have a full line of open-front panties, from glow-in-the-dark lacy crotchless versions to the Lycra Strappy Crotchless Panty. (Lots of outdoor clothing is made with Lycra.) They also have a broad selection of vibrators, strap-ons, videos, pleasure kits, and lots more.
- *Executive Affairs.* The graphics on the website are well designed and not distracting—you can actually concentrate on the words! It gives a clear description of the products and then directs you to "Select a Category of Pleasure": dongs and dildos, vibrators, bondage, sensual jewelry—you get the point.

## Those Extra Outdoor Necessities

REI (Recreational Equipment Incorporated) has just about everything you need for a positive camping experience. They can outfit everyone from the weekend warrior to the hard-core athlete. You probably already know about the fifty or so REI stores nationwide. But if there's none right down the street from you, you can take advantage of their very convenient online shopping service. Their website links to several of the brand names they carry and gives thorough descriptions of lots of their merchandise. (See Resources.)

REI has a great selection of those cute little camping lanterns. For years I thought they were a froufrou luxury that I could certainly live without. Then I got one. What had I been thinking? It's not like they're that expensive or take up an enormous amount of room. They're sturdy and safer than candles, and they shed a lot of light.

The Mini Candle Lantern is adorable, burns for up to six hours, and stands four inches high. What more could you need? For those with longer staying power (the longer the candle glow, the brighter the afterglow, right?), you can get an eight-hour aluminum lantern. Or you can really go all out and get a brass one. (See Chapter 3 for setting-the-mood suggestions, and see Resources for product information.)

Outdoor Research, the accessory specialists, has come up with a few things that ease the job of packing. Their Outdoor Organizer is a rugged, practical carrying pouch that's perfect for organizing and protecting smaller items, from toiletries to camping accessories. Its full-zip closure provides quick access to your gear yet keeps small items safely tucked inside—no matter how rough the terrain. All the little pouches, pockets, and compartments will enable you to keep things separate and find them in the dark, without having to paw through everything. Although OR probably wasn't thinking of this at the design meeting, it is also the perfect pouch for accoutrements specific to sexual needs: condoms, dildos, extra batteries, massage creams, scarves, French ticklers, penis pumps, and whatever else works for you. It's a handy-dandy waterproof pouch.

OR also makes a Woman's Travel Kit. "Our customers asked for it, and we've delivered," says the catalog. It contains shampoo, conditioner, deodorant, body lotion, body soap, and makeup removal wipes, and there's plenty of room for tampons, pads, and condoms. Most OR stuff is available at REI and many other sports specialists.

Another handy little item to have is a lightweight picnic blanket. LL Bean calls theirs a Wool Picnic Throw, and Design Salt's is an Outdoor Blanket. But you can call it your "why don't we do it in the bush" blanket. LL Bean's Wool Picnic Throw is sixty square inches of waterproof latex on the back with a wool front. Nylon web carry straps are attached for quick get-aways.

Design Salt's Outdoor Blanket is a blanket and a ground cloth all in one. One side is coated nylon to prevent moisture from seeping from the ground below; the other side is fleece that's both fast drying (that's important) and gentle on your bare bottom. Its stuff sack converts to a pillow—which can come in very handy.

These companies thought they were designing picnic blankets, but—ha!—we've got bigger and better plans for these little ground covers.

The planning you do for a trip is essential, so you might want to check out guidebooks for your particular destination. Adventurous Traveler Bookstore is a great place to start. Simply dial 1-800-282-3963. Tell them where you want to go, and they'll tell you what book you need (in addition to this one, of course) to give you the most pertinent information.

# Chapter 2

---

## THE LOVE DEN

> *Sex in a pup tent.*
> *Condensation drips slowly.*
> *Water in my eyes.*
> — ALISON HERSCHBERG

Sometimes your outdoor lovin' will take place in a shelter of some kind. It could be a tent, a bivy sack, or even a hammock. In order to carry out your love tryst in private, you can create shelter in various ways. As long as you have a willing partner and the proper equipment, the possibilities are endless. It's nice to know your options ahead of time so you can be best prepared for whatever opportunities come your way. This chapter lays out a few of these options.

If you're going for the real cushy sort of place, like one with a bed, I've even got a few secrets about our fair Forest Service and other such caretakers of our pristine forestlands.

# The Love Palace

Before you get out in the woods, you need to get the right tent. When purchasing a tent, people often overlook color. They shop for size, shape, weight, and so on, but not many think of color. In the store it might not seem to matter. But consider the color that will be reflected through your tent in the morning light. Choose a warm color like red, beige, yellow, or amber for at least the top half of your tent. As the morning sun penetrates the tent, you and your loved one will be bathed in warm, dreamy skin tones, as opposed to harsh cold blue light.

Beyond color, don't cheap out on the tent. A leaky, flimsy tent can ruin not only your night but your whole trip. There are several good brands out there—North Face, Sierra Design, Marmot, and Kelty to name a few. Buy one. Be sure to ask whether the tent has features that make it water-proof, windproof, and bugproof. A good tent will have a rain fly, internal pouches, and hooks or straps inside on which to hang things. It is also important to check the size of the tent. It should be big enough for two people and have a place (either under the rain fly or inside the tent) for your packs.

And don't forget the vestibule! Vestibule? A vestibule is an extended rain fly that creates an enclosed entryway out-side the tent. Vestibules are great for wet shoes, packs, the dog, or to cook under if it's raining. North Face, Eureka, and most other quality tent companies make them.

Fester wasn't a real big camper and hadn't thought about the aforementioned necessary features on a tent. On his way to Martha's Vineyard with his girlfriend, Jane, he picked up a cheap sixty-nine-dollar one. They took a cab to the campground and found their spot. As they set up the new tent, which they quickly realized was too small, Jane sheepishly admitted that she had forgotten to pack the air mattress. "Okay, we'll use our ponchos as a ground cloth," grumbled Fester. They got the tent up—just as the sky let loose. Because there was barely enough room for the two of them, the packs had to stay outside in the rain under Fester's poncho. What a guy!

He was awakened at four A.M. by a river running through his sleeping bag. Meanwhile, his poncho was outside. Jane, who had forgotten the air mattresses, was high and dry sleeping on her poncho. At that point he moved into her sleeping bag. Room or not, he was coming in.

The next day it only took twelve quarters to dry his sleeping bag. Fester's parting words: "Don't cheap out on the tent." But even with a good tent, this can still happen if you don't trench the tent and put a ground cloth down.

## Where to Set Up?

Once you arrive at your campsite, consider where you will set up your love den. In most cases it is best to place your tent on a flat, level surface. Slope would not only affect your sleep, it could also add an unwanted dimension to your presleep activity. Gravity always wins! If you have to be on an incline, keep your head higher than your feet. Even for the most balanced of lovers, however, a slope can be disorienting.

It's convenient to camp near a drinking and washing water source, for several reasons: You won't have to carry all your water with you, you'll have a place for bathing, and water supplies great ambience. Furthermore, the sounds of moving water may help mask your love groans.

Remember to take the weather into account. Pay attention to where water will run if it happens to rain while you're in slumber. You'll want a place sheltered from the wind and howling rains. Trees often serve as good protection, and besides, among trees you are more likely to find firewood.

If you find a spot that looks like it's been used a lot as a campsite, use it. It's better to overuse one spot than to lightly mess up the whole forest. But if some other party has already taken what you think is an ideal spot, tough! They got there first. Go find another spot far enough away for both their privacy and yours.

Now that you've purchased the tent with the color so warm, selected the homestead, and found a spot you like, you need to build your love palace. The temptation is to become a human squeegee and scrape the entire area clear of all debris with the side of your hiking boot. Don't do it. As you get down on all fours and lift pine cones, sticks, and stones out with your bare hands, you may impress your intended by your concern for the natural environment, but it's better to leave leaves and pine needles in place. Not only does ground cover participate in the natural protection against erosion of the forest floor, it also provides a porous, absorbent means for keeping standing water away from your tent. This natural blanket is not only softer than dirt, it's cleaner than the dirt below. Your ground cloth won't get so filthy, and you will be perceived as a low-impact lover. What I mean is, you will create a low impact on the environment, leaving the forest pristine for future lovers.

---

### IS IT BEDTIME YET?

Once you have your tent ideally placed and set up, you'll want to know how much longer before you can commence your nighttime activities. Look to the sun to calculate the hours left of daylight. Here's how to use the "hands of time":

1. Hold your hand up at arm's length, with the pinkie along the horizon.
2. Count the number of hands (four fingers only)

between the horizon and the bottom edge of
the sun.

3. Each hand counts for one hour, with each finger
being fifteen minutes.

Try it. It's accurate to within seven minutes.

---

## Huggin' in a Hammock

Hammocks are associated with lazing around reading or
bird watching, right? But the added dimension of hanging
free and swinging in the breeze while loving on your
sweetie has great appeal too. Tom Ness and Sophia Sparks
think so, and through their company, New Tribe, they have
made the Treeboat, a hammock specifically designed with
the happy lovemaking couple in mind. Its four indepen-
dent shrouds give the Treeboat stability and make it nearly
impossible to capsize. With all the frolicking you'll be
doing, that's an important feature. This rugged portable
bed is six feet long and thirty inches wide and is made of
tough nylon canvas, renowned for its strength and abrasion
resistance. The slip-in battens at each end will keep the two
of you from rolling into each other yet let you stay close.

When I asked Tom if the Treeboat had been field-tested
for our intended purpose, he assured me himself that his
hammock has played the field and has successfully scored
high. He did, however, warn that you might want to put a
sheet on the hammock before any major activity. "With that
much exposed skin rubbing directly on the hammock," he
said, "you may chafe or rug-burn your bum."

New Tribe has really gotten into this hammock thing.
They also have an insulative Cozy that ties along the outside
bottom to keep in the heat. They make several kinds of
mosquito nets so you won't be bugged while up in the tree.

Tom described in great detail the various methods of
Treeboat sexual contact and their advantages. In New

Tribe's catalog two people are shown lying on their backs with their heads at opposite ends of the hammock, facing each other with their legs entwined. This position puts each person's hands conveniently on the other's genitalia. The couple slide into each other because the Treeboat has one center of gravity. It offers limitless possibilities for positions for oral sex as well. Tantric sex is a wonderful way to use it for intercourse.

## Tantric Sex

Tantric sex is a method of touching the spirit as well as the body. The goal is to prolong sexual arousal—not to climax quickly but to enjoy the pleasure as long as possible. (Tantric sex is described in the *Kama Sutra* as an ancient Indian tradition.) The belief is that prolonging sex will not only enhance the sex act but allow time for deeper communication and mutual understanding. You can have Tantric sex over a several-day period, in which you slowly remove clothing and veils of privacy as you expose yourself without reservation.

You could start by remaining clothed and just relaxing and talking openly. Then later as you sit naked facing each other, progress to the basic strokes. Lightly stroke everywhere but the breasts and genitals. Then lie next to each other and feel the presence of each other's body. Do not have intercourse yet. Sit up face-to-face, and lightly massage and stroke the genitals and breasts. The penis can slowly enter the vagina a little at a time.

The man enters his partner in a half-erect state and keeps it that way. If the penis gets too hard, it wants to flip around in the wrong direction, and you will need to change position, or you could be very uncomfortable in a big hurry. If the man can successfully stay half-hard, he can stay in for a long time because the genitals are comfortably pressed together. Control orgasm with slow movements or by pulling down on the testicles. When you are both ready, you can trigger orgasm with a predetermined movement or muscle squeeze.

## Doggie in a Hammock

A good way to engage in old-fashioned energetic sex is doggie style. The female needs to hold on to the battens at one end of the hammock. You will both want a pillow under your knees. Once you get into the groove, so to speak, you can get the hammock going in a nice end-to-end rocking (hobbyhorse style). Try this position close to the ground until you get the hang of it. Sexual bliss can reduce a person's judgment, and you wouldn't want any mishaps ten feet up.

### Cushion Your Hammock

To soften the hammock surface, you can purchase a hammock pad that ties onto the corners. I saw one at Brookstone called the Reversible Sunbrella Hammock Pad. It was expensive, of course, but it was cushy solid green on one side and had green and white stripes on the other. If you are the least bit handy, you could simply sew a few straps or ribbons onto the corners of a sheet. That improvisation could cost you five bucks and about a half hour's time. Brookstone also has a Reversible Sunbrella Pillow, which is about three feet wide and fastens with a loop and hook straps.

## We Need a Bivy, Baby

A bivouac is an emergency campsite. You create it when you have wandered off the trail and are lost, or when the weather gets really lousy in a hurry and you can't get to your destination. In those cases you use whatever you have available to make yourselves comfortable and protected. From this original definition, a bivy sac has evolved into a lightweight tentlike sleeping-bag cover.

Outdoor Research makes an Advanced Double Bivy Sack. For those of you looking for an ultralightweight housing unit, OR once again has saved the day (or night). Their two-person bivy sack is lighter than any two-person tent and represents a new era in ultralight two-person shelters. Not only is OR's Double Bivy bigger than two sleeping bags that zip together, but it will keep you dry—from the rain anyway. What you do to make yourselves wet from the inside is your business.

Widely known in the outdoor industry as the "love shack," the Double Bivy is simply a longer, wider, and taller version of the one-person Advanced Bivy. It has all kinds of features: a permanently attached no-see-um netting, two internal zippered stash pockets (to keep your "personals" close at hand), and two sets of straps to keep your sleeping-pads in place during amorous activity. It is an excellent two person shelter for mountaineering, bike touring, sea kayaking, self-supported whitewater trips, adventure travel, and most important, having sex privately without having to lug a big heavy tent around.

In a pinch, you may have to construct an old-fashioned lean-to. This is simply a one-sided shelter made with five poles or branches and a cover. Put it together like this:

1. Set two poles upright about eight feet apart. (Existing trees work great.) Lash two more poles diagonally to these, extending about four to five feet, depending on how much headroom you need.
2. Lash a fifth pole, or even a rope, across, joining the two uprights at the diagonal poles.

3. The roof can be made with a tarp, poncho, or vegetation, depending on what's available and how resourceful you are.
4. Position your lean-to appropriately, to shade you from sun, block the wind, or keep the rain from diluting your coffee.

---

### GETTING FOUND

Since you are out in the woods with your snuggle buddy, you may want to get lost on purpose. But if you get lost accidentally, a few general guidelines can help you get found before you build a lean-to or set up a bivouac situation.

1. Try to retrace your steps.
2. Stay out of the wind.
3. Don't panic.
4. Look for signs that will help you get your bearings such as a streambed, trail, or road.
5. Huddle together for warmth. (I always have your best intimate interests at heart.)

---

Eddie, a Forest Service ranger, routinely parked his big green pickup truck at the head of a particular abandoned trail to scout the area. One drizzly day he returned from his mission to discover a note tucked under the wiper blade. The note read, "Apparently, this trail isn't as abandoned as we thought. We are up here, we are safe, and we would rather not be disturbed." The note was signed, "Two Hugging Hikers."

Had there been no note, Eddie would have simply gotten into his truck and driven off. Since he had now been alerted that there was "life up in them thar hills," he felt it his responsibility to make sure this wasn't some kind of decoy note, as in a Meryl Streep and Kevin Bacon movie.

He quietly hiked a ways up the trail and glimpsed two bodies flailing in what appeared to be a consensual manner under a lean-to. He quickly backed away down the hill and radioed on a loudspeaker from the truck. The couple grunted him an okay. Off he drove, thinking, "Now, there's a couple who really follows regulations. They let the authorities know they were in the wilderness." A few miles down the road he thought, "Maybe I'll bring my wife up here this summer!"

# Getting High in the Woods

Bet you thought this section was going to be about drugs, huh? Wrong! But now that I have your attention, I'd like to give you the benefits and (mostly) the pitfalls of setting up your tent at high altitudes. When hiking at very high altitudes, it is highly recommended that you set up a base camp at a lower elevation and take day hikes up into the stratosphere. This sort of arrangement has a couple of advantages.

Having a base camp at a lower elevation means you don't have to carry all your stuff up into the high hills. You also have the added convenience of being able to breathe and have sex at the same time without passing out. Oh, you didn't know this could be a problem? Okay, let me explain how breathing, sex, and altitude are connected.

Each cell in your body needs oxygen to burn nutrients and make energy. Due to lower air pressure at higher altitudes (8,000 to 10,000 feet), about thirty percent less oxygen is available than at sea level. This can result in labored breathing, and make hills seem steeper and distances feel longer. The adage "sleep low, hike high" is appropriate, and even more so when you are planning on having sex before bed. According to Dr. Tim, "High altitude can make you feel light-headed, especially during times of increased oxygen demand," like when you are having sex. It may give you a quick orgasmic rush, but over the long haul, breathing could become difficult. You will need all the available oxygen you can get to make it through those last few humps. So sleep (and have sex) at lower altitudes, and take day hikes up into the clouds.

I don't mean to put a wet blanket on your fun. Even though the percentage of oxygen in the air is the same at a higher altitude as at sea level, the decrease in air pressure means there's less oxygen in your blood, so less oxygen reaches the cells that need it. This can result in a condition called hypoxia, a deficiency of oxygen reaching the tissues of the body.

## Dehydration

While I'm on the topic of the body's responses, let's talk about water. Blood, like everything else in your body, is mostly water. If you don't drink enough water, your blood will get thicker, and it will have much more difficulty moving the nutrients, waste, and everything in it to get where it needs to go. No matter what altitude you are in, you sweat out a lot of water while hiking and having sex (which, of course, are your two primary activities in the woods). You need to replace this lost water. Without it you won't be able to do either activity very well, and that wouldn't be good at all. On such strenuous-activity days, it is recommended you drink three to four quarts of water.

### Grand Teton Oral Express

Judy and Sam were hiking in the Grand Tetons. (Hiking in a place called "Big Tits" could put anyone in a penis-throbbing mood.) As they approached their planned destination, they found it too populated for their liking. After a swig of water and three seconds of deliberation, they decided to continue their ascent up to Amphitheater Lake, which was at a considerably higher altitude.

Once they were in the privacy of their own lake, Judy proceeded to "service" Sam in the manner he enjoyed. It could have been the altitude, or maybe it was the setting, but for some reason the light-headedness of the head on his shoulders gave way to an extraordinarily delightful explosion of his *other* head. Now, many years later, Sam still gets a little twinge when Judy offers him a "Grand Teton."

## Forest Service at Your Service . . .

John Muir (1838–1914), the American explorer, naturalist, and writer, crusaded for the creation of national parks and the conservation of natural resources in the late 1800s and helped persuade President Theodore Roosevelt to set aside nearly 148 million acres of forest reserves. Since this land is owned by the U.S. government and the people of the United States (that's us), we're allowed to have sex in it, right? I doubt that is the specific activity John Muir had in mind, but sex often falls under the category of outdoor recreation, so we can surmise that he would be pleased with our conclusion.

The Forest Service was established in 1905 to provide for the conversation and best use of the forest resources in the United States. Today it is responsible for 191 million acres in the United States, Puerto Rico, and the Virgin Islands. (You can have a lot of sex in 191 million acres!) The service conducts research into forest.y, the use of forest products, and wild-land management.

Many parks and forests have interpretive centers that provide visitors with information about the natural and anthropological history of the area. The centers are also forthcoming with maps, trail information, flood warnings, fire danger alerts, mosquito meters, and litter bags.

"This is all very interesting," you might be asking, "but

what does it have to do with love dens?" Hang tight, I'm getting to it.

Believe it or not, having sex in the woods does not always have to mean warding off insects, fighting with large critters, and sleeping on lumpy pine-cone-studded surfaces. You can actually enjoy the great outdoors indoors. Check out obsolete fire lookouts, ranger stations, and guard stations. Many years ago these structures were built in national forests to house workers and allow them to perform their intended duties. People worked as fire lookouts, and rangers conducted forest research and oversaw woodland activities. Now some of these structures have outlived their initial purposes, but they often are quite functional and have intrinsic historical value. In order to preserve them, the Forest Service has made several of these facilities available for the public to rent.

Some of the shelters might be somewhat tricky to find, so when you are looking for one, be prepared to follow your map closely. Will it be worth it? You bet. By definition, what could have a more romantic, panoramic view than a fire lookout, which is placed specifically to offer the best vantage point of an entire forest?

Two books will help make this treasure hunt a little easier. Both of them discuss how to make reservations, how to get to each location, what's available at each site, and how long you can stay.

• *How to Rent a Fire Lookout in the Pacific Northwest* by Tom Foley and Tish Steinfeld. It describes sleeping facilities available in Oregon and Washington. Only devotion to duty keeps Foley and Steinfeld writing when they could be savoring the sites described in this "guide to renting fire lookouts, guard stations, ranger cabins, warming shelters and bunkhouses in the National Forests of Oregon and Washington."

- *Firetowers, Lookouts, and Rustic Cabins for Rent* by Carolyne Ilona Gatesy. This book also discusses the hows and wheres of alternative outdoor sleeping facilities. It describes those available in California, Oregon, Washington, Utah, Wyoming, Idaho, Montana, and Nevada.

Both books, along with a number of others that will aid you in your quest for the perfect outdoor vacation, are available through Mountaineers Bookstore and elsewhere. (See Resources.)

If you are a member of the Mountaineers Club, you can also rent space in a lodge. The Mountaineers have five lodges in the Pacific Northwest available to members only. If you are a member or are interested in becoming one, give them a call.

For you East Coasters, the Potomac Appalachian Trail Club (PATC) has cabins available for rent. They will send you a complete information guide with photos showing all the cabins in the PATC system. To rent a cabin, contact PATC using the information in Resources.

Michael, a former Forest Service employee and shameless punster, gave me the following information and suggestions: "The Mountaineers publish a great northwest almanac that lists addresses and phone numbers for Forest Service and Park Service ranger stations in the Northwest. These contact numbers would be helpful to lovers planning outings or 'innings' in the woods. Obtaining a little local information on regulations and the likely whereabouts of rangers and other tourists can save 'em-bare-ass-ment.' What appears to be a remote spot could be the weekly site of a guided tour. Sometimes there is limited access to sensitive spots—I mean fragile habitat—or restrictions because of recent bear activity. Ask at the local ranger station about regulations and good places for solitude before slipping into the bush."

Michael stayed at several fire lookouts before they became available for rent. At that time they had beds, canned and dry food, tables, and propane and/or wood stoves. None of them were architectural gems, he said, but the solitude, views, and protection from the elements made them well worth the trip. Now, you supply your own food, but the rest is pretty much the same. Many of the fire lookouts have been preserved by volunteer efforts. Michael's personal contribution was to pack in a toilet seat for an outhouse. That's one way to be king of the hill—carry your own throne!

# Chapter 3

*"Come quickly, I am tasting stars!"*
—DOM PÉRIGNON *(1638–1715), at the moment of his discovery of champagne*

## The Wine and the Meal

Dom Pérignon knew the intoxicating effect of a star-studded sky, coupled with a few swigs of a refreshing adult beverage. Granted, the finest gourmet wine or champagne would be the most impressive option to pull out of your hat as you serve an elegant camp dinner. But if you carry a big, heavy wine bottle all the way up the mountain, you have to carry the empty all the way down. The pack-it-in, pack-it-out rule definitely applies. But have no fear! There are some (almost as) posh alternatives. Ever try wine-in-a-box? When properly handled, it can be just as intoxicating and even alluring. You may not be toting the finest French Bordeaux, and you certainly won't find Dom Pérignon in a cardboard box, but hey, you are in the woods, and certain compromises are expected from even the most demanding lover.

Pour this lustrous liquid into your plastic wineglass, your sierra cup, or your cereal bowl, then remove the box from your table or ground cloth. You don't want a constant reminder that your glistening nectar-of-the-gods came from a container that looks suspiciously like a box of cheap crackers.

The advantages of this sort of container are twofold, however, and certainly outweigh its questionable reputation. First, the box is burnable, never to be seen or, more important, carried again. Second, the "bag" inside is a practical, sturdy receptacle made of a strong, durable material called Mylar. You have to figure that if this bag safely held wine, it can certainly be used as a container for other liquids. It never hurts to have a spare water bottle, particularly if you and your mate find yourselves a little more dehydrated than usual on the "morning after" your wine-and-sex party.

Plus, this bag has an airtight spout, right? (You can make this assumption as long as the wine didn't leak out into your backpack.) Since it holds air, it can be used as a pillow. With the night you have planned ahead, a spare pillow might come in very handy. Who knows what kind of acrobatics might ensue?

But remember that it is important to keep your strength up for what's to come. Along with the vino, be sure to include some actual nourishment. Resist the temptation to have a liquid dinner.

## Horrible Hangovers

If you do find that you have overindulged in wine or some other libation, there are a few actions you can take before bedding down for the night. Go for a walk with your companion. This will let the alcohol work its way through your system, while you enjoy the stars and the fresh outdoors in the captivating company of your chosen partner. Just make sure the two of you don't get lost.

Drink lots of water before you sleep. Alcohol has a dehydrating effect on our bodies, which is the main contributor to the next day's hangover. Aspirin, taken before the headache, truly does help prevent a throbbing head. Take two before bed, and don't call me in the morning. I've heard that aspirin placed firmly between the knees is an effective form of birth control, but it's actually more effective in preventing a hangover.

## Nip O' Liquor

There's nothing like a little nip of brandy or an after-dinner apéritif of cognac or Amaretto to warm your cockles in the chilly night air. But think of your container. Forget about glass—I'm not sure which would be worst: the broken glass, the sticky mess, or the loss of lustrous liquid. However you slice it, or in this case pour it, use an unbreakable container. Long ago I learned to transport distilled libations into the woods in either a plastic or stainless steel flask.

## "Honey, What's for Dinner?"

> *"The way to a man's heart is through his stomach."*
> —ANONYMOUS (*popular wisdom*)

> *"Anybody who believes that the way to a man's heart is through his stomach flunked geography."*
> —ROBERT BYRNE

Take your pick on the quotes, but no matter which suits you, you've got to be really horny to perceive Spam and a Snickers bar as a romantic gourmet meal. Like having sex in the woods, cooking in the woods can be an exhilarating, creative activity. And if you do it right, it can be every bit as satisfying as lovemaking.

Whether you're car camping, taking an extensive river trip, or backpacking, the answer to the question "What's for dinner?" could make or break your chances for intimacy within the next several hours. This is your time to show off and shine.

Car camping obviously gives you the greatest culinary possibilities, in that you theoretically could bring anything from a refrigerator to a gas grill. River camping also has few limitations if you do it right.

Gloria was dating one of those "Mama, don't let your babies grow up to be rafters" river guides. After a glorious day of shooting tumultuous rapids, lying on the shore for a midday romp, and skinny-dipping under crystal-clear waterfalls, Wayde felt it was time to set up camp for the night. After they selected the perfect site, they began unloading the boat. Out came the cooler full of fresh vegetables, beer and wine, the folding table, and what seemed like two five-hundred-pound Dutch ovens.

Totally prepared to overwhelm and impress his intended, Wayde set up the folding table and began chopping, cutting, and most important, lighting a small bed of coals. Being the outdoor Galloping Gourmet that he is, he soon had the following menu prepared:

### HORS D'OEUVRES
*Grilled oysters*
*Baked Brie on crispy rounds*
*Chardonnay*

### ENTRÉE
*Fresh baked sausage lasagna*
*Arugula and mixed salad greens, topped with
Gorgonzola and walnuts, and a raspberry
vinaigrette dressing*

### DESSERT
*Chocolate cake with raspberries,
topped with homemade vanilla ice cream
(none of that dehydrated ice cream packed in
tin foil for this Don Juan)*

The secret here is the Dutch oven. At carside or riverside, you can be a hero if you follow a few simple rules. For one ten-inch oven, basically you need about ten to fifteen coals that are good and glowing red hot. Set the oven on seven or eight of the coals, and distribute the rest evenly on the lid of the oven. You may need to adjust the number of coals depending on the outside temperature, the wind, and the warmth of the sand. Also remember that for Dutch oven cooking you use about one-third to one-half less water than the recipe requires.

To get even heat with a Dutch oven, you put two-thirds of the coals on the top. Since heat rises, all the heat from the bottom coals go up. About half the heat from the top coals radiates down, so you get an even heat. If you put most of the coals on the bottom, you'll burn the bottom and the top will be cool. In general use more coals (twenty to twenty-five) for heavy foods like meat, and fewer (twelve to fifteen) for more delicate cakes and pastries.

Oh, you don't want to lug a one-hundred-pound Dutch oven up a mountain? Whimp! Cascade Design has a great line of backpacking cookware sold under its Traveling Light logo. Look for Outback Ovens and Evolution Cookware to convert your camp stove into a temperature-controlled oven for gourmet backcountry cooking and baking. They can be found at most outdoor outfitters.

Let's try these recipes on for size:

---

## *Lasagna*

### INGREDIENTS

1 can or jar (12 to 16 ounces) of tomato sauce
Spinach (1 bag, cleaned)
½ pound dry lasagna noodles, uncooked
½ cup ricotta cheese

½ cup cottage cheese
Cooked sausage (optional)
1 cup water

1. Build a couple layers of each of the ingredients, starting with a layer of sauce, then spinach, dry lasagna
   noodles, and cheeses.
2. After it's all built, pour in 1 cup of water.
3. Cover.
4. Set the Dutch oven on 7 or 8 hot coals.
5. Place 12 to 14 coals on top.
6. Cook for about an hour.

---

## Oysters, Grilled or Raw

*Oysters have long been considered an aphrodesiac, possibly because
of the chemicals that make up the oyster itself. The more likely reason is that oysters resemble erogenous parts of the female body. If you
camp on the beach, oysters may be an easy item to obtain. But they
also will keep in a cooler or a cool pack for a day. I don't know
about you, but I like my oysters raw—with a squirt of lemon. Oysters also taste great grilled on foil with a little butter, garlic, and soy
sauce. But then again, what doesn't taste good grilled with butter,
garlic, and soy sauce?*

---

## Chocolate Cake with Raspberries

### INGREDIENTS

Box of chocolate cake mix
Frozen raspberries or canned pie filling (optional)

1. Follow the instructions on the cake box, but use only two-thirds the amount of required water.
2. Butter the bottom and sides of the Dutch oven.
3. Pour in the cake mix.
4. Set the oven on 5 or 6 coals, with 8 to 10 on top.
5. When you can smell the cake, it's done, usually after about 25 minutes.
6. To make it fancy, use frozen raspberries or canned pie filling for the top after the cake is cooked.

---

### Vanilla Ice Cream

This handmade method is sure to impress. If you can freeze ice cream with your very own hands, imagine what other magic those hands can perform.

#### INGREDIENTS TO MIX AHEAD OF TIME

1 cup heavy cream
1 teaspoons vanilla
2 eggs
1 cup milk

#### ADDITIONAL INGREDIENTS

2 sandwich-size Ziploc bags
2 cups crushed ice
1 cup salt

1. Place the ice and ½ cup salt in one Ziploc bag.
2. Pour the premixed ingredients into the other bag, and zip it tight.
3. Place the cream bag inside the ice bag.
4. Mix and massage the ice bag in your hands. Work the

cream until it turns to ice cream. You will probably
need the other ½ cup salt after a few minutes.
5. Place the ice cream on the chocolate cake.

*Mmm*—creamy homemade ice cream over hot chocolate
cake with raspberries! It doesn't get any better!

To top it all off, Wayde performed all this culinary magic
dressed in a bow tie and apron—nice touch. We won't ask
what else he had on.

---

## One Ripe Avocado

Lucy was shopping for her camp-out with Brian. In the produce section of the grocery store, as she reached for an avocado, she noticed a little sticker on it indicating its ripeness.
She got a devilish little flash in her head and removed the
sticker. Then she placed the avocado in her shopping cart.

Later in the tent, after a long day's hike and a satisfying
Mexican meal, Lucy and Brian settled into their zip-
together sleeping bags. Things started heating up as the
two began pawing and playing. When Brian reached down
to explore, he felt a foreign object tangled in Lucy's pubic
hair. She had a hard time containing her laughter as Brian
reached for a flashlight to investigate. The avocado sticker
was stuck prominently in place. It read "Ready to Eat."

---

## Enchiladas

### INGREDIENTS

6–8 corn tortilla shells
1 cup refried beans
½ cup onions, chopped

1 pound chicken, precooked
½ cup cheddar cheese, shredded
¼ cup sour cream
1 cup salsa
Olives, to taste

1. Line the bottom and sides of a Dutch oven with tortilla shells.
2. Layer with beans, onions, chicken, and cheese.
3. Set the oven on 4 or 5 coals, with 2 or 3 coals on top.
4. Cook for about ½ hour.
5. Serve with sour cream, salsa, and olives.

---

Burritos are easy to prepare when you don't have the luxury of a Dutch oven. They are a great one-item meal. Tortilla shells pack really well, you can roll up any number of your Mexican ingredients, and they can even be their own plate, so you have fewer dishes to do.

---

### *Burritos*

#### INGREDIENTS

6–8 flour tortillas
2 tablespoons butter
½ cup onions, chopped
1 red or green pepper, chopped
½ pound shredded beef
1 cup refried beans
¼ cup sour cream
½ cup cheddar cheese, shredded
1 jalapeño pepper, chopped
1 bunch cilantro

1 tomato, diced
1 avocado, sliced

1. Wrap the tortilla shells in foil and warm for 5 minutes over fire.
2. Sauté the tortillas in the butter, onions, pepper, and beef.
3. Add the beans and stir.
4. Place each tortilla on a plate or napkin. Coat with the sour cream and cheese. Spread the bean mixture. Top with the jalapeño, cilantro, tomato, and avocado.
5. Fold to enclose, and serve.

### Spice Up Dinner—Not Your Fingers!

If you wish to spice up your meal with fresh jalapeño peppers, watch out. The fumes can get into your lungs and eyes and cause a general nuisance. That's bad, although you can certainly live with it. But the hotness of the juices and especially the seeds will stay on your hands for a long time—well after your feeble attempts to wash it off. You know how you're not supposed to rub your eyes after you've been cutting jalapeños? Well, eyes aren't the only mucous membranes that are sensitive to hot pepper juices.

Yep, you guessed it. On another camping trip Lucy prepared a delicious Mexican meal for herself and Brian: tacos, guacamole, the works. Jalapeños were everywhere—including on Lucy's hands. Later, she hopped in the sack, thinking Brian was coming right away. A few minutes went by, but no Brian. Lucy figured she'd prime her own pump while waiting for him. As soon as she reached down and mixed her peppered fingers with the juices of her private parts, she knew she'd made a big mistake. Poor Lucy was hot, all right—she was smokin'!

## *Grilled Salmon and Pesto Linguini*

### INGREDIENTS

1 pound salmon
1 lemon, sliced
½ pound linguini noodles
½ cup pesto

1. Set a grill on top of hot coals. (Your oven rack from home works great for camp grilling.)
2. Coat salmon with half the pesto and lemon slices.
3. Wrap salmon in foil and set on grill.
4. Boil the noodles.
5. When done, drain them and mix with the remaining pesto.
6. Serve salmon over bed of pesto noodles.

On a longer trip, smoked salmon makes a great treat. It comes vacuum-packed and needs no refrigeration.

## *Cinnamon Rolls*

After the night you had, you both will need something hearty. How about hot fresh cinnamon rolls for breakfast?

### INGREDIENTS

1 tube Pillsbury frozen white bread dough
1 tablespoon cinnamon

2 tablespoons butter
¼ cup sugar

1. Roll out the bread dough on wax paper.
2. Sprinkle with cinnamon, butter, and sugar.
3. Roll up the dough like a long sausage (not as long as last night's, of course).
4. Slice it into little round disks.
5. Butter the inside of the Dutch oven, both the bottom and sides.
6. Pack the cinnamon roll disks along the bottom. Add more butter and cinnamon.
7. Cover the oven. Set it on 5 or 6 coals, and place 8 to 10 on top.
8. You know they're done when you can smell them. (An added benefit to this recipe is that the frozen bread dough thaws out during the day, keeping the cooler cold. As it thaws, the dough also starts rising.)

## Erotic Cocktails

Any sexual experience can be enhanced by the perfect cocktail, to complement foreplay or refresh you afterward. A Thermos full of drinks could be just the thing to make your romantic evening in the woods perfect. Here are some recipes for erotic cocktails to whip out when the mood strikes, wherever that may be:

---

*S e x   o n   t h e   B e a c h*

¾ oz. peach schnapps
¾ oz. vodka
Cranberry juice
Orange juice

1. Combine the peach schnapps and vodka in a tall glass.
2. Fill with half cranberry and half orange juice.

Variation: To make a Sex on the Beach Doggie Style, just add a cocktail weinie on a toothpick.

———————————

### *S a t i n   B r e e z e*

My friend Sue and I made up this drink while bartending back in our youth. The satin was the sheets where *amore*—Amaretto—happens. The warm balmy breeze was the tropical flavors of the rum and orange juice. These are actually quite tasty—try one.

¾ oz. Amaretto
¾ oz. rum
Orange juice

1. Combine the Amaretto and rum.
2. Add orange juice as desired.

———————————

### *S l o w   C o m f o r t a b l e   S c r e w*

¾ oz. sloe gin
¾ oz. Southern Comfort
¾ oz. vodka

1. Pour the ingredients into a tall glass.
2. Fill with orange juice.

———————————

### *O r g a s m*

½ oz. Kahlua
½ oz. Bailey's Irish Cream

½ oz. Amaretto
½ oz. vodka
Heavy cream

1. Pour the ingredients into a tall glass.
2. Fill with cream, and shake.

———————————

*S e a b r e e z e*

1¼ oz. vodka
Cranberry juice
Grapefruit juice

1. Pour the vodka into a highball glass.
2. Fill with half cranberry and half grapefruit juice.

———————————

*T e q u i l a   S u n s e t*

1½ oz. tequila
Pineapple juice
Grenadine

1. Add the pineapple juice to the tequila.
2. Add a splash of grenadine.
3. Pour slowly into a highball glass. Do not shake.

These drink recipes came straight from the *Professional Bartenders School of New England Guide,* 19th ed. For further information, call 1-888-437-4657 (or 1-888-4DRINKS).

# Creative Camping Cookbooks

Several cookbooks are available that offer delicious outdoor culinary delights. For the hard-core backpacker, I strongly suggest *NOLS Cookery.* NOLS stands for National Outdoor Leadership School, and as the name implies, they are the leaders when it comes to living and thriving in the great outdoors. Their best-selling outdoor cookbook features 170 creative recipes for two to four persons, plus information on nutrition, menu planning, packing, and more, including some tricks with aluminum pans. It also has mouthwatering recipes made with dehydrated and lightweight food.

Another little camp cookbook full of good recipes and ideas is *Basic Essentials of Cooking in the Outdoors* by Cliff Jacobson, part of the Basic Essentials series. The delightful *Totally Camping Cookbook,* by Helene Siegel and Karen Gillingham, focuses more on cooking good food outdoors than on packing a backpack efficiently or airdropping a cache of food onto the tundra. (See Resources.)

## Ambience

Something's missing from our romantic setting: flowers and candlelight. They would set the mood just perfectly, but it's unlikely that you'll bring along your leaded crystal vase. I recommend that you make a vase out of aluminum foil. Show off your sculpting techniques *and* add ambience all in one fell swoop. The flowers, of course, will have to be seasonal.

One great way to improvise a candleholder is to set the candle in a plastic bag. Well, don't just put it in an empty bag. First you put a little dirt in the bag, to give it a little weight. Then you fuss with it until it stands up by itself. The bag supplies a great stand in which to house a candle.

And of course you brought the tablecloth—a lightweight cloth or plastic tablecloth comes in very handy in the woods. This may sound like a frivolous item, but a tablecloth could easily be the only layer that separates you from the ground, or from other people's nasty tabletop escapades. If you don't get it all messy with dinner, you could also use it as an extra layer of ground cloth or cover-up after the sun sets.

## Mouth-Altering Snacks

While we're discussing oral consumables, a couple of snacks are great to keep handy for when you are parched or when your mouth needs a change of venue. Lemon drops will get you right in the sour buds, thus creating saliva just when you need it. If other parts of our bodies could salivate on command (or with the insertion of a lemon drop), the world would be a happier place.

Coffee nips have often saved the day. They not only give you a little jolt; they offer something to suck on. And your suck muscles will appreciate the workout to get them in shape for later.

If you want a bit of a jolt, chocolate-covered espresso beans take the cake. Three or four of those babies are stronger than a double latte. You'll be running up that trail, or climbing up your partner—depending on the time of day. I do want to warn you, though, that they are straight caffeine, so if consuming caffeine after four P.M. keeps you up all night, check your watch before popping your snack.

### Edible Novelties

Among the more interesting woodland consumables are the following.

- Edible condoms—Not too good for protection, but they make a great snack
- Whipped cream—Body dessert topping
- Edible undies—Eat the clothes right off your partner. Choose from cherry, pink champagne, piña colada, passion fruit, and strawberry flavors.

To impress Italian lovers, use Penis Pasta and Boobs Pasta to add a little sexual energy to your next spaghetti meal. I've seen them in a few different stores. They're very silly, and seven bucks is totally overpriced for a pound of pasta. But hey, people pay a high price for humor, sex, and novelty—Penis Pasta and Boobs Pasta have all three! Don't be a wet noodle, try some!

**Attack of the Aphrodisiac**

Truffles and other mushrooms look like penises, and oysters look like vaginas. But will eating them make you crave and desire their look-a-likes? That is a question that scientists, chefs, sex therapists, and kings have been pondering for years. I've yet to discover an aphrodisiac that truly causes blood to flow to our relevant organs.

But if you *think* a grapefruit is going to get you off—it will! Powdered rhinoceros horn is commonly considered an aphrodisiac, but it has no more substantiated evidence of success than any other. The mind is a powerful thing. When you are already feeling amorous and the juices are flowing, almost anything can tip the scale. The most amateur *Penthouse* Forum letter may do the trick. But if sex is the farthest thing from your mind, it will take more than a mushroom or a grapefruit to get you going.

# There's Nothing Romantic About *Giardia*

*Giardia lamblia* is a microscopic organism that finds its way into the digestive systems, and inadvertently the feces, of woodland creatures. *Giardia* is also referred to as Beaver Fever. It is unclear whether this protozoon has a deleterious effect on animals in the wild, but it certainly does on humans. And personally, I'm not going to follow a beaver around for a few weeks to see if it suffers from severe projectile diarrhea, putrefying flatulence, abdominal bloating, dehydration, weakness, and malaise. But if this same beaver, be it sick or merely a carrier, drops his or her load upstream from your romantic woodland hideaway, in a short week or two you could be losing it in more ways than you'd care to count. As with using proper birth control, an ounce of prevention is worth a pound of cure.

Although it's not as romantic as wine, water is an essential item on any camper's list. Boiling water means instant death for any *giardia*, bacteria, and viruses it contains. It is recommended that you boil water for ten minutes at sea level. At high altitudes, with their woods just perfect for sex playgrounds, water boils at a lower temperature, so you'll need to boil it longer up there. One minute per thousand feet seems to be the going rate. Since this boiling method uses a lot of fuel and takes a long time, you should know about some alternative ways to combat or prevent *giardia*.

### Acidophilus

If you do get *giardia*, the good news is that it eventually does clear up. You could, however, speed things along, decrease the symptoms, and possibly prevent it altogether by taking acidophilus. Acidophilus creates an unfavorable environment for *giardia* in your intestines. It can also help with symptoms of diarrhea caused by too much fruit, nervousness about possible upcoming sex, or whatever else causes diarrhea. Acidophilus tablets come in several chewable flavors (with blueberry receiving the highest rating, in a totally informal poll).

Karen contracted *giardia* while she was pregnant and living in a Third World country. Consuming large amounts of acidophilus helped decrease her *giardia* discomfort tenfold. She recovered, and her horrible bout with *giardia* didn't affect the baby at all. (As an aside, the baby had to be born by cesarean section. Medical practices being what they were in that country, they cut the baby only a little bit, behind his ear, at birth. Unable to pass up a humorous opportunity, his parents named him Nick!)

### Go Iodine!

Iodine kills bacteria, viruses, and *giardia*. Go iodine! Whether you use the tablets, crystals, or liquid to purify water, iodine is safe for humans and unsafe for all those other little irritants. Granted, the iodine gives the water a somewhat medicinelike odor and taste, but it is well worth it. Note, though, that pregnant women and people with thyroid conditions should consult their physicians before consuming water that has been purified with iodine.

Like some relationships, iodine has a shelf life. Consider it the petunias and geraniums of your camping gear— annuals that need to be purchased every spring. Iodine pills shouldn't break the bank. They cost about five dollars for a bottle that will treat fifty quarts of water.

### Other Water Purifiers

Liquid chlorine bleach is a cheap, manageable water purifier. Just add two drops per quart of clear water, or four drops per quart of very cold or cloudy water. After thirty minutes your water will be suitable for drinking.

Water filters can be purchased for anywhere from $25 to $250. Only a 4-micron filter is necessary to trap *giardia*, monsters that they are. Bacteria squeeze through that, but they will get trapped in a 2-micron filter. Viruses, a fraction of the size of bacteria, are unstoppable by any filter. If you are holding your rendezvous in the Third World, you will want to incorporate an iodine treatment along with your filter system.

When purchasing a water filter, check the speed at which it filters water, how quickly its filter will clog, and how easy it is to clean. Some people are more susceptible to water demons than others, but by taking a few precautions and by using a little common sense, your trip is likely to proceed smoothly, at least as far as the water is concerned.

# Chapter 4

> *Tickle me with pine.*
> *I douse you with repellent.*
> *Wilderness foreplay.*
> —ALISON HERSCHBERG

## Setting the Mood

Woodland foreplay, like most facets of life, has an order to it. Contrary to what most men believe (or at least all too often seem to practice), "Are you ready yet?" is not the ultimate mood inducer. Men, I know this is hard for you to hear, but after all those years of wordlessly groping in the dark, I've got to give it to you straight: Foreplay doesn't begin when you're lying down, in the dark, zipped into the bag, and listening to the deafening chirp of the crickets as your heart pounds and you're wondering whether the only other person in the tent is as horny and hopeful as you are.

Foreplay began when you were back in the car, on the trail, on the river, when you were smelling the flowers and nibbling the back of her neck as she picked berries, cradling her buttocks affectionately as she scrambled up a hill—are you catching on?

# The Romantic Fire

"You play with fire, you get burned!" was my grandmother's untimely warning to each of her married daughters upon the announcement of conception.

Fire has been associated with romance from the beginning of time. Cuddling by a warm campfire ignites the fires that kindle love's burning embers.

Before you indulge in the intoxicating benefits of such pyro-delights, be properly prepared. The two of you will drift off into never-never land with greater ease if you have gathered all the necessary campfire materials in advance and readied your site appropriately. First, make a pile of tinder: teeny-tiny burnables like paper, dry grass, wood shavings, cattail heads, and belly-button lint. In a separate pile, stash your kindling: small sticks, burnable litter, and other combustibles. Then collect heavier logs and large wood chunks, which will keep your fire going with little maintenance. By the time you have a good strong fire, you're not going to want to be bothered tending it.

One good trick is to drag a dead tree to your campsite, then whittle away at it as the night progresses. Even in the most picked-over campground, all you need to do is to walk a little farther than everyone else has—which usually isn't that far—to find plenty of wood for the evening. Or buy a bundle of firewood on your way to the camp area. At most parks it is forbidden to cut down anything standing—dead or alive.

Before you create the optimal romantic fire, you need to find out the campground rules. Are you even allowed to build a campfire in this area? Nothing cools hot erotic embers faster than some Ranger Rick type appearing on the scene. When Smokey and Jen had finally finished cleaning up the "mess hall," they were snuggling by the fire, cheeks aglow from wine, weather, wind, and warm tingly feelings. But they were shaken from their bliss when Mr.

Ranger (squeaky white teeth, tacky khaki Forest Service shorts, crisp shirt, hat, and shiny badge) approached them with a disapproving scowl. He caught them tightly entwined wearing fewer articles of clothing than they had worn at dinner. They grimaced quasi-apologetically as they got the lecture—"fire danger" this, and "fire-free forest" that. "We're sorry, sir; thank you, sir; we'll put it out right away." Don't let violations of the rules cool your mood!

## Site Prep

To build the best possible fire, you must find the best site. The ground should be level and clear of small burnables like pine needles, grass, twigs, and dry leaves—blanket-singeing sparks can also ignite your surroundings.

Build your fire close to where you will be sleeping. Once you've gotten yourselves in the mood, you're not going to want to stumble far in the dark to lay yourselves down. A long walk to your bed leaves room for possible woodland disasters: You could trip and fall in your passion and haste; you could get lost; and worse, a tumble through the woods could cool the mood irreconcilably. None of these risks are worth taking.

If possible, find a log to serve as a movable bench for two. It's nice to lower your buns into a warm seat by the fire with your main squeeze. You and your partner will also appreciate being able to move out of the smoke should the wind shift.

Don't get so overzealous that you make the fire bigger than you'll want to deal with as your amorous mood kicks in. Once you're up to the heavy-sighing stage and close to clothing removal, resist the temptation to add that huge tree stump to your fire. Chances are you'll soon have your hands full with another huge stump and won't want a blazing campfire to interfere with your internal fires.

Be careful about what you use for a snuggle blanket near

the campfire. Elmer thought his sleeping bag would make a really comfortable cushion for stargazing and campfire snuggling. Thinking he was the only one who could make sparks fly that evening, he hadn't thought about those little fireworks that come shooting out of even the most expertly built campfire (which he deemed his to be). By the time he and Myrtle were cuddling in his love nest, the sleeping bag resembled Swiss cheese and was barely usable. The next morning when he held it up to the cold light of day, he could practically make constellations from all the little holes.

---

The fires of passion are part of our daily speech. Bet you've used some of these phrases. Do any others come to mind?
- Burning with desire
- We be smokin'
- When you're hot, you're hot
- One hot mama
- "Come on, baby, light my fire"—the Doors
- Too hot to handle
- Hot pants
- Hot to trot
- Hot and heavy
- Got the hots

---

**Elements of Fire**

Just as lovemaking needs a heat source, fuel, and oxygen, so too does firemaking. Here are some suggestions.

- *Heat.* Keep a butane lighter, magnesium block and striker, or magnifying glass and paper on hand, or use waterproof matches.
- *Fuel.* Collect your fuel before the sun goes down. (Groping around in the dark is an activity

reserved for inside the tent, not for looking for sticks outside.)
- *Oxygen.* Blow on the fire (to get those lips and cheek muscles warmed up for the night ahead).

# Basics of Body Massage

After a long hard day of fun and exercise, there's nothing quite like a relaxing yet stimulating body massage. The following Swedish massage basics are merely suggestions. You will, I suspect, vary your moves according to your own style and the moans and groans of your partner. Massage can be either a loving way to help your partner relax or an erotic prelude to sex play. Indulge yourselves. Take advantage of your solitude and of the long night ahead.

### Oils and Lotions

Use a luxurious pleasant-smelling oil or lotion. Countless varieties of massage oils are on the market. But if you will be in your $300 all-weather sleeping bag, take heed: Massage oils don't give up their hold on fabric without a fight. Using the oil would feel good for the moment, but you would have to live with (and sleep with) the consequences for a long time. Instead, use a junky blanket, towel, or sheet that can be easily washed. You could even make a sleeping bag liner by sewing a couple of flannel sheets together.

I find lotion to be a perfectly acceptable alternative to the slippery staining oils. Like oils, several good lotions are on the market. (See Resources.) Myo-Ther is a silky non-staining massage lotion used by massage therapists. It's greaseless, odorless, doesn't promote bacterial growth, and washes out in a regular wash cycle.

A completely dripless solution is the Lush Massage Bar, which you can hold in the palm of your hand. It comes in various sizes, shapes, and flavors, with names such as

Therapy, Ego, Snake Oil Bar, and Cherie Ripe. The bars are made with cocoa butter, shea butter, lavender oil, and perfumes.

To use a Lush Massage Bar, hold it in your palm and glide it over your lover's skin, leaving a slight silky lubricating film. The coating allows your fingers to effortlessly work their magic—without the mess of an oil or lotion.

The massage bar has several advantages. It doesn't drip. There's no bottle to try to open with slippery fingers or worry about spilling. It doesn't leave your skin so totally slicked with oil that you feel like a greased pig. And it feels and smells delightful!

If you are in serious bear country, keep your use of fragrant accoutrements to a minimum. Bears may be attracted to perfumes, including deodorant! One way to keep bears from interrupting your evening is to make your campsite as fragrance free as possible.

## Basic Strokes

There are five basic strokes to Swedish body massage. One way to give someone a whole body massage is to do all these strokes sequentially. Complete the whole sequence in one area and then move on to another area, where you begin the entire sequence again.

*Effleurage* (long smooth strokes). Effleurage is the introductory movement, the first to be done on each part of the body. Place both hands on the body, at the point closest to you. Glide toward the center of the body. Move toward the heart, and apply deep pressure. Return your hands to the starting position with light pressure, keeping contact with the body. Effleurage is very relaxing and at the same time nourishing to the body. It increases the flow of blood from the periphery to the center. (Increased blood flow will be important as the night progresses.)

*Compression movements* (petrissage, friction, and vibration). Now comes the squeezing and rubbing action. These movements should be progressive: Apply them lightly at first, then gradually increase the pressure. People can tolerate more pressure over thick fleshy areas like the buttocks, but areas of thin tissue like the penis or the bony surfaces right on the spine can't take it. Don't press so hard that the muscles get tight. Compression movements help prevent the stiffness of recently exercised muscles—perfect after a day of hiking, climbing, or skiing.

*Petrissage* means "kneading," like you do with bread dough. Pick up the skin, and roll it around as you squeeze it.

When you use friction strokes, your hands slip along the skin, making small circles with your thumb and fingertips. Three friction movements are:

- *Chucking.* Firmly grab a limb with both hands. Move your hands together and apart without taking them from the surface.
- *Wringing.* Hold the limb and wring it gently like a washrag.
- *Vibration.* Press your hands on the area and shake them uncontrollably.

*Tapotement* (percussionlike movements). Tapotement is a percussion movement that stimulates the nerves, blood flow, and muscle tone. Relax your wrists and quickly alternate the movement of your fingers. A few types are:

- Beating with closed fists
- Hacking with the baby-finger side of your hands
- Cupping with raised knuckles
- Tapping with fingertips only
- Slapping with the flat part of your hand

*Joint movements.* Make sure your partner is relaxed while you gently manipulate his or her joints. Pay extra attention to knees and ankles.

*Nerve strokes* (very light tickles). This part brings chills even in the hottest of climates. Move your fingertips out from the center of the body in light motions. Trail down the body to calm and soothe it. Nerve strokes are a good way to let your partner know that you're about to end the massage.

These basic movements are well worth practicing at home. If you do, you'll really have something to show off out in the woods, where all the senses are heightened. As master masseur or masseuse, you will be able to effortlessly help your partner totally relax (and physical relaxation certainly facilitates sexual arousal). But don't expect to receive a massage the same night you give one. The recipient may like to savor being indulged without immediately having to reciprocate.

And don't expect your partner to always want to make love after a massage, especially if he or she has had a big day. Massage can often be a way of connecting physically and expressing your love, without intercourse or orgasm. During or after the massage, your lover may drop off to sleep (but wake up in a very loving mood in the morning or middle of the night!).

---

### SOCK TIP

You'll enjoy your massage more if your feet are warm. (Can't get cold feet about having sex in the woods.) Keep a pair of clean socks in your sleeping bag. Once your toes are toasty, stick the socks back into the bag so they'll be ready for the next evening's escapades.

---

# From Swedish to the Sensual

Massage can serve to awaken as well as to relax, since enlivening the senses definitely awakens sexual instincts. My massage instructor complains, "Every time I try to practice new massage techniques on my husband, it quickly and invariably turns to sex."

Erotic massage often stimulates by starting with the "tease." How well you tease depends on how well you know your partner and your skills at working the contours of the human body. The tease plays on the boundary between Swedish massage and sensual massage. Beginning with the tactile pleasures of the Swedish, work toward the sensuality of the erotic.

For example, make broad strokes from the shoulders, using circular motions, working toward the lower back. Using petrissage strokes, knead the skin like bread dough as you work the deep tissue of the buttocks. Continue with large strokes along the back of the thigh, and use feathered nerve strokes up the inner thigh.

Use the broad, firm effleurage strokes to work the larger muscles of the back and shoulders. Then gently move up to just below the ear and down the front of the neck to the top of the chest. As you approach the sensitive area of the breasts and the nipples, lightly brush. Depending on your partner's response, introduce the sensation of your warm breath and moist lips.

# Music

Nothing enhances the mood quite like soft music subtly wafting through the air. If you are car camping, several simple mood enhancers are available that would otherwise be too cumbersome to lug up a mountain. A portable CD–boom box will do the trick. Just make sure you have extra batteries and CDs. Don't be tempted to use the car battery—it can die. Using the old-dead-battery excuse to stay in the woods longer is one thing; actually having a dead battery in the woods is quite another—and it certainly isn't cute.

## Worlds Away

You techno-radio nerds can get an AM radio to do some pretty impressive things. Tell your date you are embarking on a trip to faraway places, pull out your AM radio, and off you go. After the sun goes down, you can often pick up radio waves from miles away. At night the ionosphere, or upper atmosphere, comes closer to the Earth, creating a big shield. It's as if we're inside a big reflective satellite dish.

Bouncing between the Earth's surface and the ionosphere, radio waves, which travel in a straight line, are able to find their way from some faraway city or foreign land to your little spot in the woods. If you're lucky, you could realistically dial in Europe, Canada, or South America.

A hand-cranked radio from the BayGen Power Group could come in handy for this endeavor. BayGen, the South African manufacturer, offers a broad line of Freeplay Self-Powered Radios, including solar-assisted models (thirty seconds of sweat equity cranking gives you an hour of power!).

Another option is the Self-Powered AM/FM Short Wave Radio by C. Crane Company. Simply crank this crank-generated radio for a few minutes, and enjoy hours of listening pleasure. Self-powered radios are available at places like Brookstone and Sharper Image. They're also featured in a variety of electronics catalogs.

As noise travels at night from other countries, it also travels to neighboring campsites. Conversations as well as music can be clearly heard a long way away. Be considerate of your neighbors' quest for woodland peace—and also watch what you say.

# Lighting Effects

If the candle lantern (see Chapter 1) is your chosen tent ambience inducer, be careful how you set up your night-stand. There's not a whole lot of room in there, so one way to set up your lantern (while conserving space) is to hang it. Most tents have little loops of webbing along the inside. You can use these loops to make an indoor clothesline with parachute cord or lightweight nylon cord. Hang your lantern in a spot that will be out of the way of flailing arms and legs. This method keeps the lantern off the tent floor, where it is likely to be kicked or knocked over.

Be forewarned: Lanterns create great shadows that can entertain passersby or onlookers for miles around. Several couples were out on a somewhat raucous camping trip. Well before all the wine and beer had been consumed, Ernest and Julia sneaked off to their tent. Later, as Bud and Henry stumbled past the couple's dimly lit tent, Henry stopped dead and tugged on Bud's sleeve. In barely audible speech he slurred, "Either that's a wine bottle, or Julia is one very lucky lady." We'll never know which.

## Battery-Powered Light

If the possibility of hot wax dripping on your back at the most inappropriate time doesn't sound like fun, you have several battery-operated illumination alternatives. Flash-lights are a great standby when it comes to producing light in a hurry. But the cold, bold incandescent light may be a little harsh for the effect you seek. A simple, cheap, color-ful solution is to change the color of your bare white light. No, I'm not suggesting you paint that tiny little flashlight bulb. You can block some of that harsh light with a variety of colored materials. One such material is theater gel, a stage trick as old as light itself (well, as old as bulbs, any-way). To give your flashlight that rock-concert colored-spotlight look, just cut out a colored transparent circle that's as big as the lens of your flashlight. Unscrew the top, and place the colored material between the rim of the flashlight and the lens so the plastic can't touch the bulb. Then screw the top back on. You can get theater gels at theater supply stores and from most stationery and arts-and-crafts supply shops. You can also use overhead transparency material, plastic wrap, or tape, available in a variety of colors.

Another product does this whole colored-lens thing for you. It's called the MagLite Accessory Pack, and it comes with a screw lid that fits most D-battery flashlights. It offers three colored lenses: red and amber for night vision, and a blue lens to penetrate smoke and fog. You can choose your filter, depending on the mood you seek to create. They retail for about ten dollars where most flashlights are sold.

Garrity Flashlights came up with an interesting way of diffusing the harsh light of a flashlight bulb. Their 2-in-1 Flashlight elongates, exposing a frosted tube.

Eveready also makes an elongating flashlight, which sets down on the wide front lens. The exposed soft-light lens in the neck comes in clear or amber, depending on the atmosphere you seek.

For you crankers, BayGen offers a self-powered lantern, which comes with a spare bulb and a 12-volt adapter. A few seconds of cranking and you're lit for the night.

## Sex for the Health of It

The fact that you are out in the woods says a lot about your desire to be fit and healthy. Whatever your chosen daytime recreation—be it hiking, boating, fishing—the real recreation could be just beginning when the sun goes down. Virginia Johnson Masters, pioneer sex researcher and cofounder of Masters and Johnson Institute, feels that a healthy sex life can improve your general physical condition. So while coital overindulgence is a good way to release the sexual energy that has built up during the day, it is also a great way to maintain health and vitality.

Beyond general health, sex has a number of specific benefits as well. It improves skin tone and color, increases blood flow, and helps skin to regenerate and become more pliable and elastic. Ejaculating on a regular basis may reduce the risk of prostate cancer in men. Sex stimulates endorphin release, which enables you to sleep more soundly and gives you a general sense of well-being. It improves muscle tone and can have a positive effect on self-image and self-esteem. It is a great cardiovascular workout—during sex the heart rate may reach 130 beats per minute. Last but not least, sex is an efficient calorie-burner. A 120-pound woman can burn 4.2 calories per minute during sex.

## Afterplay

A chapter on foreplay would be somewhat incomplete without mention of afterplay. While your senses are heightened, you can lie totally still and silent, taking in the nighttime gifts that the woods have to offer. Smell the cool night air, listen to the chirping crickets, and enjoy the stars, as you feel your heart rates return to their calm state.

As you recount the day and the fulfillment you've just experienced, tent talk replaces your bedroom pillow talk. Thank each other with light postcoital strokes and reassuring hugs.

## Mess Management

How to keep the lovemaking mess to a minimum and what to do with said mess when you're through is as much a part of the experience as the climax (well, almost as much). When I posed my mess management query to various individuals, they made the following suggestions. At their request, the contributors of these trade secrets shall remain nameless:

- Swallow, don't spit. You're not at the dentist.
- If you do more in than out, you'll make less of a wet spot.
- Ziplocs were made for sex mess.
- What mess? We like to get each other all slimy and let it dry.
- That stuff sticks to the tent wall—use a Kleenex.
- If you're rimming or engaging in anal play, go for the baby wipes and Saran Wrap. And take a swig of Listerine, just in case. (Rimming—mouth-anal contact—can spread disease carried in the feces such as hepatitis and intestinal parasites. Scrub up really well and use plastic wrap or dental dams so both of your bottoms can enjoy tender, relaxing pleasure.)
- Put one of those big blue hospital pads right in the sleeping bag. It's absorbent on one side, waterproof on the other—perfect.
- Wear a minipad the next day to catch anything you've missed.

Now that you know how to create the perfect mood before sex in the woods, and how to clean up the mess when you're finished, you can turn off the flashlight, pull up the covers, and snuggle into woodland slumber.

# Chapter 5

*"Just because you're in the wilderness is no reason to behave like a savage."*

—RICHARD WILSON

Even the most pristine individuals may lower their standards for cleanliness when they are in the woods. At the wilderness edge some of us undergo a shift in acceptability of what we'll eat, what we'll let others see us do, and how bad we let ourselves smell. Somehow the oft-partnered combination of modesty and cleanliness goes right out the window.

As a mild example, let's say you drop a pancake on the ground. Rather than discard the innocent pancake, you let the pine needles serve as a welcome garnish. Mostly out of necessity, personal hygiene and cleanliness standards also decrease. Your body, however, is still your temple, and if you are hoping for visitors into said shrine, you will want to take heed of a few of these woodland tips and suggestions.

## The Perfect Towel

In *The Hitchhiker's Guide to the Galaxy*, the character Ford Perfect seemed to feel that a towel is about the most massively useful thing an interstellar hitchhiker can have. He used his largish bath towel for warmth as he bounded across the cold moons of Jaglan Beta, as a sail on a miniraft cruising down the slow River Moth, as a wet weapon in hand-to-hand combat, and to get himself out of a number of intergalactic jams.

Ford Perfect probably didn't know about the convenient features of the PackTowl by Cascade Designs. This light-weight, quick-drying cloth is designed for the outdoors. Made of a synthetic fiber called Viscose, the PackTowl holds nine times its weight in water. With just a squeeze you can wring out 90 percent of the liquid it's holding. A twenty-by-forty-inch PackTowl can dry your bum, wipe your brow, or dry your dishes. In a pinch, it could sop up the wet spot in your postcoital bliss just prior to slumber. Outdoor Research even has a small PackTowl as a standard inclusion in some of its kitchen kits. If you have your towel, you can handle just about anything.

If you don't have a PackTowl, a chamois makes a great alternative, but it's not nearly as high tech.

## Toothbrushing

Many people feel that camping is a vacation from many daily routines: the telephone, cars, traffic, screaming kids, fax machines—you get my drift. Many also perceive camp-ing as a time to vacation from oral hygiene. They may even purposefully leave their toothbrush at home.

Not brushing is not only unsanitary, it's totally gross. If you have any hopes or prospects for woodland hanky-panky, you will not follow this practice. Assuming, and hoping, that you aren't a nonbrushing lowlife, there are a few things you may want to know about outdoor brushing.

A dry pasteless toothbrush actually removes more plaque than a wet pasty one. Honest, just ask your dentist. I recommend doing the dry brush thing first, then using a little bit of paste and water as a follow-up. To rinse, use what I call the blow-and-spray method: Fill your cheeks with air, then spray the wet slime out of your mouth. That way you disperse the toothpaste thinly over a wider area. It washes away faster and makes less of an environmental and aesthetic impact.

To rinse off the brush, you need only a little bit of water, not gallons. Think about this when you're at home, too, and leave the water running unnecessarily as you diligently buff your tusks.

As a backup to brushing, or in case you unexpectedly find yourself close enough to kiss, you have several options from which to choose. Arm and Hammer Toothpaste Gum is a good choice. No, it doesn't taste like you're chewing on a salty sandbox—it's actually quite refreshing. You'll find it in the toothpaste section of most pharmacies and grocery stores.

They're no substitute for brushing, of course, but Altoids are a great breath adjuster. These "curiously strong peppermint" mints come in a great little tin that could come in quite handy later for things like OBs or other tampons without applicators, latex gloves, small lube tubes—that kind of stuff. Another even stronger great-tasting breath mint is the Starbucks After Coffee mint. These tiny little tablets are so strong, even Rosie O'Donnell can't pop more than one at a time in her mouth. When they're all gone, you're left with another handy tin, about half the size of the Altoid one— just perfect for condoms and French ticklers.

### Halls Cough Job

Speaking of altering your breath, Halls Menthol Cough Drops not only suppress coughs, they also give you good, tingly, minty breath. As Diane was prepping to hop in the sleeping bag, she felt a slight cold coming on, so she popped a Halls in her mouth. Since she didn't want to pass her possible cold on to Chip, she offered him oral favors to help rest his weary body. Well, much to his surprise and delight, the menthol gave more than her breath that tingly feeling! Oh baby, oh baby! Try Altoids and Starbucks mints. They work, too!

Diane mentioned this new discovery to a friend of hers. (Got to pass along good tricks, you know.) When the friend's husband met Chip, he exuberantly shook his hand and said, "Hi, Chip, it's great to meet you. You are a very lucky man!" Women can get lucky with this method, too. Just have your man pop that cough drop in before he pleasures you.

## Soap

Dr. Bronner's 18-in-1 Pure Castile Soap is the classic camper's soap for several reasons. You can use it to shave, shampoo, and brush your teeth. It is environmentally friendly and biodegradable, contains no phosphates, and gets you clean! Dr. Bronner's comes in several flavors and scents. Most are benign and just clean you without fanfare. But heed my warning! If you are planning to wash your personals, don't use the peppermint flavor. It burns like hell!

Another woods-worthy soap is an all-purpose cleaner for travelers called Travel Suds. I first saw it as a standard item in the Outdoor Research Travel Kit. It works great as a soap and shampoo and to do spot laundry (should you create any spots that need laundering before you get home). It's biodegradable. And best of all, it doesn't sting when used on mucous-membrane-type locations!

# Shavin' Heaven

For those men who do want to shave in the woods, the Outdoor Research Travel Kit I just mentioned (with the Travel Suds) is an ideal item. The kit has a hook so you can hang it from a tree, and a mirror is Velcro-ed to the middle of it. With all your shaving needs hanging at your fingertips, it's like being right in your own bathroom. (But you won't have to worry about the mirror fogging up.)

# Keep It Clean

"No crotch rot for this girl," I overheard an avid outdoorswoman proclaim. In the woods you probably don't have the luxury of the daily shower, and you can certainly forget about the double-jet Jacuzzi or bubble bath. So what's a woman to do? One of this woman's tricks is to stay on top of the issue and don't let things get out of hand. What she was trying to say is that some way or another, make sure you wash yourself every day. If you have a river at your disposal, you don't have much to worry about—except, of course, glacially cold water. As chilly as that may sound, a few minutes of "chilling out" far surpasses discomfort, chafing, and attracting flies.

Oh, you don't have a river at your campsite? Thanks to the wonders of modern convenience and Johnson & Johnson, baby wipes can keep things fresh and kissingly clean. After all, there's nothing softer and sweeter than a baby's behind, right? Your behind might at least try for second place.

Alcohol preps were suggested to accomplish this task. Although they are pretty good at getting you clean, they hardly make the grade as far as taste and fragrance go.

---

### FERTILIZING PHOSPHATES

Phosphates aren't really poisonous. Are you ready for a little science lesson? What makes phosphates harmful to the environment is that they act like fertilizer. This fertilizer causes an excessive amount of algae growth in the water. The excess algae actually choke out fish.

---

**The SunShower**

The SunShower by Basic Designs is a black bag that heats water using solar power. Simply fill it with water, and lay it in a sunny but private spot if you're feeling modest. As you heat up and get all grimy throughout the day, your shower also heats up, eagerly anticipating your arrival. Aside from the possibility of being clean after a long day in the woods, the SunShower also offers many romantic possibilities.

Harry, who was not very astute in the romance division, for once had a romantic idea and was psyched to put it into action. In the morning he diligently filled the SunShower and laid it out to receive maximum sun exposure all day. He and his wife, Josie, were heading for an exhilarating, exhausting day in the woods. He lusted all day long, thinking about how good that hot shower and his clean naked wife would feel upon their return.

After their long day of hiking, Harry was going to blindfold Josie to give her a little surprise. Then he would walk her over to the shower and slowly disrobe her of her sweaty, salty play clothes piece by piece. As he hiked behind her during the day, he plotted which piece he'd remove first. He'd start with her T-shirt, leaving on the bra (as he liked seeing the lace against her sweaty skin). Then he'd remove her socks and sneaks—he wanted to soap and massage her hot, tired feet. The shorts would be next. Then he'd slowly go for the panties. He shuddered at the thought of gently tugging her black lacy panties over her curved buttocks. He was set to lather every nook and cranny and rinse her and himself off with the hot SunShower water.

At the end of their hike, the hot and sweaty Josie, totally oblivious to Harry's plan, was thinking she'd better take a shower before Harry used up all the hot water, as he usually did. She saw the SunShower and without hesitation hung it, disrobed, hopped under it, and scrubbed away the day. When she was finished, she considerately refilled the shower bag from the icy river and hung it in the chilly late-afternoon sun.

# Deodorant

Deodorant is something you don't usually associate with sex unless someone fails to use it. Rancid pits may attract mosquitoes, but they may sure keep romance at further than arm's length. Something people complain about almost as often as deadly pits is sickening-smelling deodorant. Years ago I found the perfect alternative.

The Crystal Stick Body Deodorant has worked wonders for me for years. It is simply what the name implies—a big ball of salt. To apply it, you moisten it and rub it around a clean pit. The salt acts as an odor absorber. Be warned, it is not an antiperspirant, so you will sweat (which some find very appealing). But you won't stink (which most find very appealing).

The Crystal Stick is particularly nice for camping because you can just wipe it on, and you're fresh for the day (or night). You can find the Crystal Stick Body Deodorant in health food stores and medium-to-high-end department stores, in the makeup or perfume department. Various brands cost anywhere from five to ten dollars and can last for well over a year, even with daily use. Crystal Stick Body Deodorant even comes as a small travel salt rock for two bucks.

# Allergies

Know before you go. If you are susceptible to grass, tree, or pollen allergies and it's not winter, be prepared. Some areas have local allergy alerts on the TV news or in the newspaper. Spring is historically the worst time for allergies. Be prepared. If antihistamines are in order, then by all means don't forget them.

# Urinary Tract Infection (UTI)

An interesting design, the human body—there's a sewer running right through a recreation area.

Wash your hands! I'm not trying to sound like a nagging mother, but when sex is in your near future, cleaning your hands is often more important than cleaning your genitals. Campers, as well as travelers, usually think they get sick from the water, but it's often due to not washing their hands thoroughly after going to the bathroom.

Jesse and her partner are avid campers. To her great disappointment, Jesse got a urinary tract infection almost every time they went camping. On the advice of her doctor, she and her partner started using individually wrapped Wet-Naps on their hands and private areas before getting intimate. Her problems were gone—no more urinary tract infections.

If you have frequent burning urination, an infection is likely. You may pass a little bit of blood in your urine, develop a fever and back pain, and have shocklike symptoms. Drinking a lot of water and cranberry juice and taking vitamin C can help a mild case. If it persists, go to a doctor for antibiotics when you get home.

Sex juices and foreign debris can get up into the urethra. Peeing as soon as possible after sex helps prevent an infection by washing some of that stuff out. If urinary tract infections are an issue for you, drinking unsweetened cranberry juice can help prevent them.

If you wear a minipad instead of using toilet paper (which is a very convenient way to go), make sure you change it a couple times a day. I know it sounds gross, but shit happens. Fecal matter near the vagina is an open invitation for a UTI.

## Yeasty Beasties

Yeast infections, affectionately known as candida, monila, or fungus, are a nuisance no matter when you get them. A trip to the woods is definitely no time to get a yeast infection. Again, be prepared!

Several things can cause a yeast infection. An oil used as a vaginal lubricant can take days to wash out, welcoming all kinds of growth. Antibiotics, pregnancy, birth-control pills, diabetes, and menstruation slightly raise the pH of the vagina, making it a little less acidic than normal. This is just right for yeast! Even semen can sometimes throw one's pH out of kilter.

When your system is out of balance, yeastlike organisms may grow quickly and cause a thick, white discharge that may look like cottage cheese and smell like baking bread. And you itch. Usually the vagina is a little too acidic for yeast to grow. (For the record, semen is slightly basic—go figure.)

In the good old days you would practically have to be airlifted out before a doctor would give you a prescription for medication. Today there are three-day over-the-counter treatments. So don't forget your Monistat!

If you're prone to yeast infections, when you're in the woods, wear loose-weave cotton underwear so your vagina can "breathe," wash thoroughly (but don't douche!) after sex, and decrease your sugar intake.

## Managing Menstruation in the Wild

No matter how you slice it, it's a drag for a woman to have her period while in the woods or at the beach. Whether you use tampons or pads, it's a good idea to keep at least a one-day supply readily available in case you get your period.

A Ziploc bag, small stuff sack, or some other small container can work well for storage. You may want to keep a reasonable stash of toilet paper and baby wipes here as well. You'll need an extra plastic bag for the used refuse, which you can't bury and certainly can't just leave behind. You might also want to take a stash of Advil or ibuprofen because, as one advertisement so wisely pointed out, "your period is more than a pain."

In 1999 Outdoor Research has come out with a Woman's Trail Kit designed specifically for women's personal needs. It has four tampons, four heavy-duty Ziploc bags, wipes, biodegradable soap, lotion, a comb, a mirror, and condoms! And there's room for minipads, Chap Stick, or other things a woman may need. As OR president Ron Gregg describes it, "This is what women have asked for—all the necessities without the foo-foo stuff."

Here's a story that I think shows the importance of being well-prepared.

*One summer four middle-aged women went out on a beach excursion. Feeling frisky and daring, they wore varying degrees of bikinis and two-piece bathing suits. All, as coincidence would have it, were experiencing menstruation. The most scantily clad of the foursome wore a black bikini and a tampon. They enjoyed a great day of fun in the sun, flirting with young men and soaking in the rays. Three hours into this experience, Ms. Black Bikini glanced down and saw that her tampon string had missed the thin bandwidth confine of her*

*bikini bottom and was flying in the breeze for all the
world to see!*

*Another of the foxy foursome had used a pad as her
device. Sometime into her day on the beach, she discovered that her suit was on wrong. She had put her leg into
the waistband, and now the sanitary napkin was totally
mislocated. If these four ladies had been considering carrying out any dalliances, they could forget it. I think it
was time for them to go home.*

## Period Sex

Having sex during your period can pose a problem even
if you are at home and have towels and a shower at your
disposal. Having sex during your period in the woods com-
pounds the problems tenfold. If it's the big, bad, heavy-flow,
I-feel-like-a-cow-giving-a-transfusion kind of evening, you
might want to skip the sex thing altogether and get a decent
night's sleep. On the days when your period is more of an
inconvenience than a discomfort, though, there are a few
alternatives to consider before making so drastic a decision
as abstinence. If the blood bothers your partner, you can tell
him that you've been wanting to try out a new oral-sex technique on him. Or you can skip the interactive part and rub
yourself to ecstasy. It's a judgment call. Remember, menstruation does not provide birth control or disease prevention,
so be sure to use condoms even when you're bleeding.

Instead is a relatively new device in menstruation management. It's a cup that holds back the flow of blood. You
simply insert it into your vagina, covering your cervix,
which is where the blood comes out. When you are at a
convenient location, like in a private spot behind a tree,
you remove and discard it. One of its appealing features for
when you're having sex is that all the blood is contained
and held back, as if you didn't have your period at all. (A

diaphragm can serve the same purpose if you have one.) You can keep an Instead in for up to twelve hours. Once you use it, simply discard it as you would a tampon or pad. In the woods, that means stick it in the Ziploc, along with used toilet tissue, creating a tidy little toss-in-the-trash pack for later.

# Chapter 6

## SEX IN THE WOODS IN OTHER PLACES

*ser•en•dip•i•ty* n: *The faculty of happening upon or making fortunate discoveries when not in search of them.*
— WEBSTER'S DICTIONARY

Sex happens! It's just a fact of life. But it seems to happen more when you're out in the wilderness. Why? Well, it could be that you're not on the phone, you're not at work, no one else is demanding your time or attention, and your stress level is decreased. It could also be that your senses are heightened, you're taking time to be with a special person, and you're relaxed and doing something fun. Sometimes friskiness, mischief, and desire can overcome all semblance of rationality—and sex happens.

The woods afford otherwise seemingly level-headed people the opportunity to indulge in things they normally only do in the privacy of their bedroom, hotel, or tent. Many enjoy having unexpected sex on the beach, in a hot spring, or on a boat. But along with this unexpected joy may come unexpected pitfalls. With a modicum of foresight and by learning from the experiences of others, you can make the most out of your outdoor escapades. This chapter contains warnings, lessons, and stories of how others have handled uncomfortable, unexpected, or potentially embarrassing situations.

# Hot Hot Springs

Hot springs are delightful natural pools that trickle up from the ground. They are designed to bring us extreme amounts of relaxing pleasure. Life doesn't get much more romantic than when soaking in 102-degree water with candlelight and the man in the moon shining his moonbeams down on two lovebirds. Follow these simple rules, and hot springs will be around for generations.

- Relax! Soak your body well.
- Never use soap—it can pollute the water for days.
- Have you ever noticed what happens when a guy cums in a hot spring (or hot tub or any water, for that matter)? The ejaculate floats to the top and takes on a really weird sticky consistency. What's happening is that semen is ejaculated as a liquid, gels immediately, then turns back to a liquid within five minutes. This is due to enzyme action and is designed to help the sperm swim upstream. So if you happen to lighten your sperm load in the water, wait a few minutes, clean it up, or fling it out of the water. It's not nice (and not all that hygienic) to leave that stuff floating around for the next people to encounter.
- Avoid vandalism, and remind others to do the same.
- Get rid of litter, whether it's yours or not.
- Don't use glass containers. Broken glass in or around the water can make you bleed.
- Heed Forest Service fire regulations.

- Be gentle on the local flora and fauna.
- Share.
- Be respectful of other bathers. Even in springs where nudity is allowed, ask before exposing your bare butt to strangers. (Not everyone feels you missed your calling as a supermodel.)
- Don't fornicate in front of others (without permission).
- Don't hang around and watch your neighbors!

## Hot Springs Solitude

Lila and Jedd had hiked all day, then made dinner, and were ready to indulge themselves in a long playful soak in Kennedy Hot Springs. They had brought candles, water, and wine in a box (can't have glass around a hot spring, you know). They had just removed their clothes, and as they soaked in complete bliss in this 102-degree water, they were easing away all the stress of the day. They had been there for about twenty minutes when Klem Kadiddlehopper came along.

"Eh, mind if I join you?" he asked. Without awaiting an answer, he removed his clothes and was in in a flash. For a while our rather disappointed couple just ignored him, hoping he'd hurry up, get relaxed, and go away. Clueless Klem never left! After a while they figured that if he was going to be rude enough to stay, then they were going to be rude enough to carry on their intended evening activities. For the longest time they very discreetly fondled each other under the water. But as the evening wore on, their interest in each other took major precedence over the presence of this interloper. They didn't come right out and do the nasty before their onlooker, but let's just say that by the end of the evening, they were both more than satisfied.

# Sex on the Beach

Fantasies seem to fall into two general categories: those you'd give anything to experience (but are probably never going to) and those that are safer or more pleasurable if they remain in your imagination.

Kevin and Lucy were in the Olympic Hot Springs in the mountains of the Pacific Northwest. They were totally engrossed in the full-moon light, playing footsie, fondling, and generally caressing each other. Somehow the topic of water sports came up (which Kevin had confided had been a fantasy of his). You know, the golden shower stuff? Without warning, Lucy slinked onto Kevin and straddled him as she started licking his ear, neck, and lips.

Then she peed on him.

She got this funny look on her face and told him what she had done. They both looked at each other in the light of the full moon and laughed as Kevin blurted, "Well, that sport is certainly overrated!"

## Tide

Although delightfully romantic and the seed of many a sex fantasy, sex on the beach is wrought with its own set of potential hazards. If you're going to have sex on an ocean beach, bear in mind that you and your lover aren't the only force of nature you will have to contend with. The tide's pull and magnetism are even more consistent than your body rhythms. In general, the tide is high and low twice a day. It takes approximately six hours to go from high to low and vice versa. For tide info, refer to a local tide chart or to the weather section of the newspaper. You could also look for indications of the tideline on the beach. One such tell-tale sign is a high-water mark—a line of seaweed, rocks, barnacles, and driftwood—that indicates that this is as high as it gets. If you plan to be positioned in one place for a while, you'd be safe to nestle in above the high-tide line. If you want to live life at the edge, perch closer to the water, but be prepared for a quick take-off.

Remember, too, that offshoot tributaries are also subject to tidal action. James and Patty were making love in the marsh grass at dusk on the Nisqually Delta. In their haste they didn't even think about the tides' effect on the delta. As their ground cloth floated up around them with the incoming tide, they got a quick oceanography lesson. They almost got out of that one dry—but not quite.

### Sand

Tides aren't the only thing to watch out for when the mood strikes on the beach. The beach is covered with a hazard for the naked body—sand. Sandpaper is sand on paper, designed to rub over something to make it smooth. Sand on the beach does the same thing. Unless you are trying to buff your bare bottom, you are advised to put a layer of something between the sand and your lovemaking body. In the heat of passion, you could rub your buns to a bright-pink pulp.

In a pinch you could spread out a towel, newspaper, or the sacrificial T-shirt. One of those lightweight picnic blankets by LL Bean or Design Salt would come in very handy at a time like this (see Chapter 1). They each have a water-proof side for the damp sand and a fabric side for your skin to keep your cheeks very happy.

What if sand gets into your tender places? Sand in an oyster is the impetus for a pearl, but sand in your oyster could be quite a nuisance. Making love outdoors increases your chances of irritants in many forms—sand, dirt, bugs, and other foreign objects—getting inside the vagina. A gynecologist suggests that urinating after sex helps flush out some of these intruders, thus aiding in the prevention of urinary tract infection. This is a good idea for sex at home, but when you're outside exposed to the elements, it's even more important. Granted, the urethra (where the pee comes out) is in the front and doesn't actually flush the vagina with liquid. But the act of squatting, peeing, and contracting the vaginal walls helps to squeeze out foreign bodies.

**Sunburn**

Any trip to the beach holds the threat of sunburn. I'm not really a proponent of tanning beds, but if you dwell in the North Country and have skin like Caspar Milquetoast, it's not a bad idea to "season" yourself before a trip to the tropics. This same recommendation applies if a nude beach is in your plans and you will be revealing the "unexposed." Sure, those golden pretanned shoulders and legs will look great. But more important, there's nothing more disappointing than spending the first night of your tropical vacation with flaming-pink breasts or a scorched penis. (Maybe that's where "too hot to handle" came from.) Actually, the high concentration of the skin pigment, melanin, in the penis protects it from burning. But you might as well get the enjoyment of coating it with a little suntan lotion.

This couple had the best intentions of protecting themselves, but as I said earlier—sex happens. Leslie and Paul were planning a big trip to Hawaii. To precondition their skin for the penetrating Hawaiian sun, they went to a tanning salon. After they received instructions for proper skin bronzing, the attendant handed them each a towel and walked away. Although two rooms were available, Leslie walked toward one and motioned Paul to follow. They closed the door behind them and both got this devilishly mischievous look on their faces. After all, it was a "bed." They were alone. And they were already very close to naked.

With hundreds of watts beaming on their bouncing buns, their bottoms got a good pre-Hawaiian tan, even if their fronts didn't.

## Overheating

"Sometimes it's just too hot to have sex on the beach!" exclaimed a woman of obvious experience. And indeed it is. If you're going to spend a day at the beach, bring plenty of water. In the unprotected beams of the relentless sun, unsuspecting lovers are easily at risk of heat exhaustion or, even worse, heat stroke.

During your beach calisthenics, the heat you generate radiates from your skin, and your body seeks to cool itself by sweating. External heat and humidity interfere with this process. With an air temperature above 90 degrees Fahrenheit, heat is dissipated mostly through the evaporation of sweat. High humidity will interfere with evaporation.

Profuse sweating and loss of fluids can lead to a shocklike condition known as heat exhaustion. It will gradually make you feel weak, tired, and generally nauseous. Heat stroke, the body's inability to control its own temperature, comes on more quickly and is very dangerous. Your breathing becomes short, and your muscles feel like they're on fire. You can even develop blurred vision and dizziness. The real danger sign is if you stop sweating. That means your primary cooling system has shut down and your temperature is skyrocketing.

If any of these things happen to either of you, don't get them confused with heightened sexual excitement! Put your extracurricular activities on hold and tend to this potentially life-threatening medical emergency. Get out of the sun, drink water, and rest. If necessary, go jump in the lake (or ocean). That'll cool you down.

**Privacy**

Some people think that the privacy of darkness will hide them. Think again.

Bob had had a glimmer of a crush on Kelly for quite a while, but she'd been unavailable until now, when they found themselves on a Mexican kayak trip with mutual friends. One night, after a few days of flirting, Bob asked Kelly if she'd accompany him for a walk on the beach. The smell of romance wafted like bacon rising up the stairs on a cold December morning. It was the kind of setting movie scenes are made of—beach, moon, stars, warm tropical breeze, waves splashing on the shore, and boy and girl hand in hand lost in the moment's perfection. (You get the picture, let's cut to the chase.)

Bob was delighted that Kelly was responsive to his advances. Soon they got to more serious foreplay. After what seemed like hours, he was suffering from a painful hard-on, but she wasn't willing to compromise her virtue—yet. She assured him she understood and wouldn't be offended if he wanted to "take care of it" on his own. He was a little disappointed but appreciated her open-mindedness. The moonlit reflection cast plenty of telltale light. Kelly smiled to herself as she watched a few quick movements and heard the *thud* of his wonder juices hitting the sand.

**Critters**

Beach creatures are fun to observe by day. But when nighttime falls, you have more important matters to see to than contending with critters, either in their live scurrying state or with their unexpected and unwelcome residue. Check ahead of time to make sure that the area where you'll be camping isn't a breeding ground, and always take precautions against bears and other critters that might make the area their home.

## Jeep Tricks

Lucy and John thought it would be romantic to sleep under the stars on the beach. They got themselves comfortable and were enjoying the sound of waves lapping on the Florida shore. Before they could get even one kiss in, however, they heard the patter of little critters all around them. At first they thought it was the turtles that run up the beach at a certain time of year, lay their eggs, and hightail it back to the water. But when they sat up, they saw the shadows of hundreds of little crabs running all around the beach. They hadn't left themselves many sleeping options other than the sand. So they had to get creative in a hurry.

The roof of the Jeep! Perfect! It was flat, free of sand, and most important at this point in time, had no crabs scurrying about.

Ah! They settled down once again, this time on the Jeep roof. Years later they both told about having the most body-shattering orgasms of their lives—and without even falling off!

## Critter Debris

Doug had graduated to the walking-cast stage of recovery from his broken ankle. He was relatively mobile, so a beach camping scene sounded reasonable. He and Lisa spent all day at a music festival, then found a secluded beachfront park just outside the city. In the dark Lisa set up the tarp in what seemed like an ideal spot, looking forward to making love to the rhythm of the waves with the cool breeze on her back. Her fantasy was shattered brusquely when she heard in the darkness, "Shit! I can't believe it! I just stepped in dogshit—with my walking cast!"

Sorry, Doug, you're on your own with this one. Good thing they had separate sleeping bags.

## SEX IN THE WATER

If there's a chance you'll be having sex *in* the water, consider these points. Water doesn't have the same effect on everyone's sexual appetite. When making love in the water, water can get rhythmically pumped into the vagina. Before you return to shore, try squeezing your vaginal muscles to force out some of the water buildup. This could help you avoid the embarrassment of an uncontrollable stream pouring down your leg as you exit the water. More important, the water can wash away the body's normal juices, causing discomfort from friction. Some like to fool around in the water, but save the main event for solid ground.

The chill of the water can work to some men's advantage. Refreshing cold water keeps some penises hard longer. But other men experience "the great disappearing penis" as soon as they hit the water. Don't take it personally—it's simply part of the scrotum's temperature-regulation process. Sperm, which is housed in the scrotum, require temperatures a few degrees colder than the rest of the body. In the cold water the scrotum shrinks up, trying to catch the warmth of the body it's attached to. Conversely, it hangs low when it's really hot out, in an attempt to get away from the body heat, to increase surface area, and keep the sperm viable.

# Sex on a Boat

You may think that being in the middle of nowhere on a boat would afford the utmost in privacy. Think again. Whether it's passengers on the boat or onlookers drifting by, be careful of the looming eyes of high-sea spies.

Terry and Tom wanted to conceive a child. It was not an unusual desire, but in their case timing was everything. Tom's job took him away for months at a time. And when he was home and the time was appropriate for an Immaculate Conception, something or someone always got in the way. On this one particular fertile occasion, Terry and Tom were on their sailboat entertaining a few well-meaning out-of-town female guests.

Unbeknownst to Tom, the girls were privy to his and Terry's wish to conceive. To help Terry, they offered to take the dinghy out to do a little exploring, leaving the twosome alone on the sailboat. Given the size of the sailboat, the old adage "If the boat's a rocking, don't bother knocking" wasn't going to work as a signal that the girls could come back aboard. So they came up with another signal. Lu slipped Terry a leopard-spotted scarf and told her to tie it on to the mast once all was quiet on the western front. The scarf trick worked, and Tom was none the wiser. A-parent-ly, it was a successful sailing trip for all involved. Baby "Gilligan" was born the next spring.

> *Can you do it on a boat?*
> *Can you do it while you float?*
> *Can you do it here or there?*
> *They can do it anywhere!*
> —LuAnn Colombo

---

It would be a long straight sail across Long Island Sound. When Sharon egged Edgar on to a midday romp on the moving sailboat, he rose to the challenge. Thinking fast on his sea legs, he tied off the tiller with a bungee cord. (He figured this one time they could have sex without it.) They played "all hands on deck" for quite a while. They never knew whether it was their bare butts bouncing or their boat weaving, but when they looked up to check on things, they were surrounded by several motorboats guiding them like a flotilla. Ahoy! Mating?

## Build Yourself a Sweaty Sauna

Few things are more relaxing or erotic than cleansing your body and soul in a hot steamy sauna. People have been steaming themselves for centuries. With a little bit of planning and ingenuity, you and your intended can steam away tension and grit quicker than you think. It may sound like a hassle, but it's quite manageable, and it'll be well worth the effort.

_Materials_

A river or lake

A clearing big enough for a fire and a tent

4 to 8 long fiberglass tent poles, threaded with shock cord

A large tarp

Fuel for a fire (see Chapter 4)

Dry rocks (not water impregnated—and don't get rocks from a stream, because they can explode like popcorn)

Balsam needles or cedar boughs

A water bottle

1. Choose a site for your sauna near water so you can jump in to chill out. Secure the tent poles in the ground, forming a dome. Make the hut big enough to avoid claustrophobia. You'll need room for two bodies and a pile of hot rocks.

2. Lay the tarp over the frame. Weigh the tarp down with other rocks. Leave a flaplike opening for you and the hot rocks.

3. Build a good hot fire outside the sauna.

4. Heat the rocks in the fire.

5. Clear an area inside the dome for the rocks. Brush away burnables, or the sauna could fill with smoke.

6. Using sticks, or a shovel, pile 6 to 10 hot rocks in the cleared area.

---

*Safety tip:* **Remember that the entryway is for you as well as the rocks, so keep the rocks away from the front door. You want to be able to escape in a hurry if things get too hot.**

---

7. Once you're settled in the dome, spread balsam needles or cedar boughs on the fire as potpourri or incense.

8. Sprinkle water on the rocks to create steam.

9. Spray water on yourselves.

10. Drink water. You don't want to dehydrate and pass out before the night gets hot.

11. Flagellate each other with leaf-laden branches to gently stimulate your skin.

12. Go jump in the lake. Wear your river sandals so you can make a beeline to the water while you're still hot. You want to get the fully stimulating effect of the hot-cold contrast against your skin. It's a great body rush.

## Whack Your Porcupine

The tarp had finally been secured, and the rocks were heating. Dave and Betsy had done everything right—left plenty of room, brought water to drink, and used cedar boughs for incense. There was even a creek right nearby. They were proud of their first sauna and very eager to indulge in it.

They stripped down naked, and after about twenty minutes of sweating, were ready for a jump in the creek.

Men, should you be inclined to hurl yourself naked into the water—beware! Without thinking, Dave climbed up on a rock overhang and took a flying leap into the water. As he did so, his poor unprotected genitalia followed suit. As he hit the water, his scrotum and penis whacked the water with a force that sent needles through his whole body.

This certainly diminished the therapeutic value of his sauna that night!

## Sex on the Way Home: From Pub to Shrub

Sometimes you're tempted to pull over on a trail or some other obvious side path. If a secluded place looks more than slightly trampled, it likely has been used as a potty stop by people and/or critters. You will probably want to move on to a less trampled area.

Richard and Lynn were out at a pub in Sheffield, England, where they tipped many a Guinness. Their stumble home seemed excruciatingly long (at least for Richard), so as they passed by Ecclesfield Park, the clearing behind the mulberry bush looked like a featherbed. Unbeknownst to either, this was the thoroughfare for the morning dog-walkers. As Richard slowly lowered Lynn down onto him, he rolled slightly to nestle into a comfortable spot. The soft, odoriferous squish that he felt under his back snapped him abruptly out of his passionate stupor.

He vowed to hold out for a bed the next time this urge emerged.

## Sex on the Golf Course: Fore! Score!

Don and Barb were on the first hole of a prestigious eighteen-hole golf course. They had just emerged from behind the bushes with a look of guilt and afterglow all over their faces. You know that look! The groundskeeper walked over to them from her cart and, with a somewhat coy smirk on her face, asked if they were scoring low. They assured her they were having a good game. As she rode off, they suspected she was thinking, "At their rate this will be a long game."

## Sex Under the Stars

Falling stars have been the recipient of secret wishes of lovers since time began. If you should be lucky enough to see one, you may want to impress your partner with the following information:

- A meteor is a dazzling streak of light in the sky, caused by sand-grain-size debris entering the Earth's atmosphere and heating up the air molecules.
- A meteor shower is seen when the Earth passes through debris left by a comet.
- Meteors aren't really falling stars, but you can still wish on them.
- There are eleven or so regular meteor showers every year.
- One such shower happens at the perfect camping time of year. The Perseid meteor showers can be viewed from about August 7 through 12. Just look in the northeastern sky from around ten P.M. to two A.M. At its peak you may see a meteor every few minutes.

**Perseid Cow Pastures**

Jim and Lucy, who had just started dating, were at a wild party. It was getting pretty late when Jim whispered to Lucy that he had a surprise for her. They got in the car, and he drove for about half an hour, not telling her where they were going. They got out of the car and started walking in the dark. With blankets and tarp in tow, they went through tall grasses, over wooden fences, and up hills. At the top of a lovely knoll, they spread out their bedding and curled up for what Lucy thought was some postparty smooching. Looking skyward, they could see star after star falling. They fell asleep making a wish on each falling star.

The next morning they awoke to find Bessy chewing her cud not four feet away. Fortunately they had dodged the cow pies in their clamber up the hill. In her still-dreamy phase-one stage of this relationship, Lucy could only think of how romantic it was that her new guy had dragged her through a cow field to watch shooting stars.

# Stand-Up Sex

On hilly terrain it's tricky to find the appropriate slope for stand-up sex. The most maneuverable position seems to be for the woman (or the shorter person) to be on the uphill side. This way, the man can negotiate his target better, and the woman's got gravity on her side. Not that she's going to impale herself on him or anything—it just works better this way. Sometimes it helps to find something to lean on!

**Big Sur**

Jen and Bill were in the woods of Big Sur, California, land of towering redwoods. Inspired by this great beauty but unprepared for activity, Bill used a redwood as his back-board. He leaned Jen against the tree, and they proceeded to make mad, passionate love. As her earth-shattering orgasm welled up inside her, Jen clutched Bill toward her, shouting, "Oh, Big Sur!" Her knees turned to Jell-O. At just that moment, their support tree cracked and fell over behind them. Good job, Big Sur. What power!

# Chapter 7

---

## PROTECTION FROM THE ELEMENTS

*The call of the wild.*
*Natural urges are strong.*
*Lay down a blue tarp.*
—ALISON HERSCHBERG

Ahh, the great outdoors—fresh air, sunshine, trees, flowers, birds, butterflies . . . poison ivy, mosquitoes, sunburn. In the balance of nature, you need a little bad to appreciate the good. But the more prepared you are for nature's ills, the less negative effect they will have on you and your fun activities.

## Nasty Nettles

A nettle is a nasty prickly plant that is often found in moist underbrush, in patches large enough to cover a ballfield. Even if you lightly brush past nettles with the back of your hand, you'll feel a light little sting, usually followed immediately by a red rash.

Nellie and Ned had been together for quite a while, but their lovemaking had been urban and limited to the bedroom. Nellie didn't want to admit to Ned how little camping experience she had, let alone her lack of outdoor sexual experiences. They went out on a lovely day hike, and Ned started getting amorous on her. Although flattered by his attention and impressed with his spontaneity, she was a little uncomfortable with the setting.

Nellie toughed it out through the blanket placement, the clothing removal, and the foreplay. Finally in the lovely warm sunshine, she was able to relax and really got into it. Her whimpers turned to groans and finally to a vocal orgasmic shudder that the whole outdoors could hear.

After their breathing returned to normal and Ned settled into snoozeland, Nellie trotted off behind some bushes to what she believed to be a safe, secluded spot. She squatted, peed, and did her Kegel exercises to squeeze out the remaining semen. She grabbed for the nearest leaves, but nervous about being exposed, she didn't notice the slight tingle. Not until she wiped off the inside of her thighs and private parts did she feel the prickly burn. Yep, poor Nellie had picked the nasty nettle!

## Poisonous Plants

Poison ivy, poison oak, and poison sumac are unassuming plants that can cause a short-lived but extremely irritating allergic form of contact dermatitis (that's a rash). This gross rash generally develops within two days of exposure and peaks after five days. It starts to decline after about a week to ten days of severe itching and general discomfort. Patches of red, itchy skin are usually followed by small blisters, which fill with a clear fluid and eventually break open, get crusty, and dry up. Not pleasant!

Poison oak, like poison ivy, is a shiny three-leaflet cluster. Both have creeping root systems and spread all over the ground, so if you see any, assume there is more and be extra cautious.

Poison ivy, poison oak, and poison sumac can be relentless. They can stay actively dormant on clothes, shoes, and camping equipment that have been stored away for months. Merely touching the leaves can expose your body to the oils, which can then be spread by touch to other parts of the body. The more sensitive the tissue, the worse the reaction can be. You can transmit it from your hands onto your food, so to avoid blisters in your mouth, wash your hands before eating. And you can transfer the big three poison resins to someone else. It would be a big drag for one person unknowingly to have the resin on his or her hands and spread it by fondling the moist sensitive regions of another. But it can happen.

Some fortunate people are not allergic to poison oak, ivy, or sumac. Lucky them. For those of you who do carry the allergy gene and are exposed, there are a few things you can do. If you touch a poison ivy or oak plant, wash with soap and water as soon as you realize you have been exposed.

Tec-labs, whose slogan is "forming a business from scratch" (clever!), make products for each stage of poison-plant discomfort. They are as follows.

- *Level 1.* Protect your skin before it's exposed: Armor is a poison oak, ivy, and sumac block.
- *Level 2.* Cleanse: Tecnu Oak-N-Ivy, a skin cleanser, gets rid of those irritating chemicals. You can use it like a soap right after you've come in contact with the nasty stuff, or even after a rash breaks out.
- *Level 3.* Relieve: CortiCool and CalaGel serve as a topical combination skin protectant, antihistamine, and anaesthetic. They relieve the itching and pain of poison oak and ivy, skin allergies, rashes, insect bites, minor burns, and minor skin irritations.

You can also use Benadryl, which comes in a topical gel and relieves the itch and reduces the scratching, allowing your body to heal more quickly.

*Caution:* **Don't take oral antihistamines if you are using an antihistamine lotion. The combination may actually make the condition worse—and you don't want that!**

### WHY DOES IT DO THAT?

Poison ivy, poison oak, and poison sumac irritate us because their leaves, stems, and roots contain the resin urushiol. Minute amounts of this stuff on exposed skin can trigger an inflammatory allergic reaction. Urushiol can be transferred by fingers or animal fur and can remain on clothing, shoes, and tools for a number of months. Scratching the rash does not spread the poison to other parts of the body but can spread the serum from the blisters, causing a secondary infection and prolonging the discomfort.

The toxin is not killed by fire and can cause severe allergic reactions internally as well as externally. If you have been exposed to or have inhaled the smoke from burning poison ivy, poison oak, or poison sumac, call your doctor.

## Hypothermia

Know about hypothermia, respect it, avoid it, and you should be fine. Hypothermia happens when your blood-pumping 98.6-degree body takes a temperature drop of even a few degrees. It can happen on a wet, chilly fifty-degree day; it doesn't need to be the dead of winter to have hypothermia sneak up on you.

Prevention is easy: Dress warm and stay dry. These precautions may seem incongruous with having sex in the outdoors, but keep it in mind. Snack on lots of high-fat and high-calorie food, and drink lots of liquids.

Shivering, one of the first signs of hypothermia, starts when your body tries to generate some heat in your muscles. Don't ignore shivers; put more clothes on. Wet clothes, especially cotton, wick away your body heat.

Make sure you have dry clothes and a blanket or sleeping bag readily available in case you become wet and sweaty after a rigorous lovemaking session. Don't do the postcoital snooze without covers nearby.

You do have another hypothermia-prevention resource: Should your hiking partner start going hypothermic, remove the clothes from the shivering one, take your own clothes off, and wrap yourself around him or her. (You knew I'd cycle back around to intimate contact, didn't you?)

Your body heat is one of your greatest resources. And of course you'll be willing to share it. This may be a tough one, but the ultimate heat transfer happens with two naked bodies in one sleeping bag. So snuggle up—doctor's orders!

## Penis Protector

Certain outdoor sports keep you hanging in the breeze. Cross-country skiing and Rollerblading come to mind. To protect them from frostbite, you may want to keep your genitals in a tidy little package, somewhat like a codpiece from days of yore. A friend of mine knit her husband a penis protector for cross-country skiing. It revolutionized the sport for him—now he can ski for hours with a hat on his "other head."

If knitting isn't your forte, you could put a wool mitten over penis and balls, or attach a felt square onto your jockstrap.

# The Old Wet Sleeping-Bag Trick, Huh?

A raft full of people, as they tried to negotiate a class-IV rapid on the Salmon River in Idaho, went flipping overboard. Everything that wasn't snugly zipped, folded, or stuffed into a dry riverbag got completely soaked, including Sharon's sleeping bag. When wet, a down-feather sleeping bag packs down nice and flat, becoming virtually useless. Being that it was late in the day, there was no way that her sleeping bag was going to be dry and fluffy warm by nightfall.

Herman, a big burly guy, had a double-wide sleeping bag (maybe because he was double wide himself). He gallantly offered to share his bag and body, to keep Sharon from catching a chill in her sleep. On the face of it, she was grateful. It wasn't until later that she had to figure out how to deal with or ignore someone else's husband's erection in the confines of one tight sleeping bag. Good luck, and good night!

# The Sun: We're Having Sun Fun Now!

When making love out in the elements, it's easy to forget to protect yourself against things like pregnancy and STDs (sexually transmitted diseases). It's even easier to forget about sunburn and dehydration.

### Sunburn

As long as you remember to take it out of the bottle and carefully cover areas exposed to the sun, sunscreen works. Sunburn stripes will show up later where spots were missed or sunscreen was applied unevenly. Be especially careful when exposing skin that usually remains covered up and out of sight. Virgin skin (skin that doesn't get exposed) is the most sensitive and vulnerable to frying in the sun. A good rule of thumb when putting on sunscreen: Have your partner help. Besides, lubricated hand-to-skin contact just sounds like a good idea, doesn't it?

Say you're on the beach. Sunscreen is supposed to follow the line of your bathing suit and go just under the cloth, in case you shift and expose that border skin. Ask your partner to pour a good amount in his or her hands and coat you well, whether an area will be exposed or not. It may be fun to have those slippery hands coat your whole derriere with good protective sunscreen.

If it's the end of the day and you feel that warm "Oh, I got too much sun" glow, you might be in trouble. Before you switch to the "Oh, I'm ready to make love" glow, soothe your burning body with cool, refreshing aloe vera gel.

Don't forget the lips! Make sure your lip balm has a sunscreen in it. Your moist ruby lips are actually a very thin sensitive layer of skin. Lips can burn, blister, and peel. Painful! Don't let this happen to you. You may need those lips for later.

## Dehydration

Drink, drink, drink! Your body can lose about three quarts of water a day through breathing, sweating, and peeing. Drink lots of water, especially if you are out hiking (or sweating for whatever reason) in hot weather.

---

*Warning:* **The sun is stronger at higher altitudes! The burning rays increase four percent per thousand feet of elevation. So if you're hiking in the hills or mountains, make sure you block out the sun.**

---

# Insects

## Mosquitoes

There are a ton of pesty bugs out there in the woods, and you don't want any of them interrupting your fun. You know the basics about mosquitoes—they suck! Blood! Yours! So you'd probably like a few pieces of information about the obnoxious creatures:

- Mosquitoes develop mostly in stagnant water, salt marshes, and other still-water environments. They are most prevalent during evening feeding time. So don't camp near a swamp. Set up camp in an open, breezy, yet secluded spot.
- Men are said to be bitten by mosquitoes more than women.
- Skin temperature and moisture (like sweat) attract mosquitoes (not good news for outdoor frolickers).
- It's mostly the carbon dioxide and lactic acid released during breathing and from your skin that attract mosquitoes.

Back in the early 1960s, a not-terribly-outdoorsy college coed aunt of mine was out on a hike with her forestry-major boyfriend. She had the big beehive hairdo and was sporting flats and pedal-pushers. Can you picture it? As they hiked along, my now-uncle charged ahead, identifying this tree and that plant while my aunt was panting behind, swatting and swearing. The problem was that her big hairdo had been lacquered into place with sticky, perfumey hairspray and served to house a great collection of no-see-em's, mosquitoes, and other flying nuisances. Not only were they attracted to the smell, but once they got in, they couldn't get out.

Moral of the story: Leave the perfumes and hairspray home. You smell great to insects just by being a stinky, sweaty human—you don't want to encourage them by smelling like flowers, too.

### Ticks

Ticks are those tiny creatures that bury their head in your skin and drink your blood. Some species carry Lyme disease and other ills. So beware, and if you get one on you, get rid of it fast. When in tick country, do at least one daily tick check. A tick check can, of course, also be a great part of foreplay. Since they burrow into warm, dark, hairy places, the first places to investigate are obvious. As you closely scrutinize the scrotum and the shaft and even peek into the head of the penis, be sure to make it as sensual as possible. For a female tick check, look very closely and investigate every fold and crease.

If the tick's head is not embedded in your skin, the first line of attack is to pluck the little suckers off with a tweezer near the head, using either gloved fingers or a commercial tick tugger. Grip low, and pull straight out in order to get the whole critter. Then wash the wound well. Don't grab the tick with bare fingers, as it may bite the hand that plucks it—yours!

If the tick's head is under the skin, smear Vaseline, butter, or another greasy substance on the affected area. This may suffocate the tick, forcing it to give up its death grip on your very tender skin, and become easily removable. Though it takes a little time, this is the safest method.

One known method of killing a burrowed tick is to spray permethrin on it and wait till it dies. Duranon Tick Repellent from Coulston contains permethrin. It is an insecticide that normally gets sprayed on clothes or inside tents and remains effective through five to ten washings. But if you have a tick on you, go for the more drastic measure—spray direct!

A few unsubstantiated rumors are circulating with regard to tick eradication: Hold a hot match on the tick (ouch!), or apply nail polish on it and let the acetone kill it. You can try these methods—they won't hurt you, but they probably won't hurt the tick either.

Lyme disease has turned up all over the United States— in the Northeast, Midwest, and Pacific Coast. The deer tick, which carries it, is tiny, so when doing a tick check, look for new "freckles." This pinhead-sized tick is usually noticeable only when engorged. A red rash around the bite will often appear three days to a month after the bite took place. You also will feel flulike symptoms (muscle aches, fatigue, fever, nausea, and so on). This very serious degenerative disease requires medical help as quickly as possible. The good news is, Lyme disease is treatable with antibiotics.

---

### NEWS FLASH! LICK LYME

At last there is a vaccine for Lyme disease. It was just developed in the fall of 1998 by researchers at the New England Medical Center in Boston. In clinical trials the vaccine was found to prevent 76 percent of cases of Lyme disease and 100 percent of cases of asymptomatic infection. Called LYMErix, the new vaccine is for patients aged fifteen to seventy. Even if you get the vaccine, don't neglect to continue your tick inspections.

---

## Black Flies

Unfortunately, black flies, like many lovers, are sunworshippers. John and Jan went backpacking and were delighted by the lack of black flies, especially given the reports they had heard. They were, however, disappointed at the drizzly, overcast weather. So they hopped into their sleeping bag and figured they'd wait out the drizzle in intimate body-clamoring style. Hours later they emerged from the tent for a hike. The sun was just peeking out from behind the clouds. They hadn't gone a hundred yards before flesh-eating black flies began pecking at them like they were hamburger. Damn!

## Why Are Bugs Biting Me?

Some insects bite because they use animal blood (like yours) to make eggs when they reproduce. Some need to drink blood to grow. Only female mosquitoes bite, so by obliterating a mosquito before she bites you, you not only save yourself, you also eradicate a whole new generation of the little monsters.

## Insect Repellents

The following are suggested guidelines for safe-sex use of insect repellents (adapted from "Suggested Guidelines for Safe Use of Insect Repellents" by the EPA):

- Apply only to exposed skin. (In your case, this could be a massive amount of skin.)
- Don't apply under clothing (unless that area will soon become exposed skin).
- Use just enough repellent to lightly cover the skin. Don't soak it in.
- Sweating increases the absorption of repellent. (Avoid sweating? Forget that!)
- Don't apply repellent to broken skin, lips, or mucous membranes. (A little bit won't kill you, but it will sure taste lousy!)

- Once you're inside, wash it off. (This may be easier said than done, unless you have a sink in your tent.)
- It is believed that repellents work by disrupting a bug's sensors. (That seems fair. They disrupt your sensual experience, you disrupt their sensors.)

Here is a review of the repellents available on the market.

***DEET.*** This broad-spectrum repellent is effective against mosquitoes, biting flies, chiggers, fleas, and ticks. It is a nasty chemical (N, N-diethyl-3-methylbenzamide, previously called N, N-diethyl-eta-toluamide for you DEET aficionados) that you wouldn't want to ingest no matter what part of your lover's body it is on. If your partner has already DEETed up for the night, you may find that you'll want to explore, fondle, and grope with your hands more than with your mouth. Avoid products with more than 30 to 35 percent DEET. This concentration is sufficient to ward off the worst hordes of bugs in the world. Higher concentrations eat up plastic watchbands and compasses. It may not harm you, but it won't help.

Each 10-degree-Celsius increase in temperature can lead to as much as a 50 percent reduction in protection time— so if things get heated up, reapply.

The 3M Company has developed a slow-release, polymer-based product containing 35 percent DEET. It is the repellent provided to U.S. military personnel and is available to the general public exclusively through the Amway Corporation, under the brand name HourGuard.

If you want lower-strength, extended-release DEET, check out Minnetonka Brands, which offers products containing 6.5 and 10 percent DEET.

Sawyer Products of Safety Harbor, Florida, makes Controlled Release DEET. The 20 percent DEET formula is encapsulated in a skin-friendly protein and comes in an eco-pump.

*Citronella.* Citronella oil, originally extracted from the grass plant *Cymbopogon nardus,* has a lemony scent. Citronella is the active ingredient in "natural" and "herbal" repellents. It is a slightly effective repellent and is not as long lasting as DEET-based products, so reapply it more often.

It's probably the smoke from citronella candles that helps keep mosquitoes away, since research has shown that people using them receive half as many bites as those who used regular candles. Besides, citronella candles smell good.

*Blocker.* Blocker is a plant-based repellent that was released in the United States in 1997. It combines soybean oil, geranium oil, and coconut oil. Studies have shown that it can give more than 97 percent protection against mosquitoes for as long as 3.5 hours after application. It's totally nontoxic and is made by Verdant Brands. Sounds like the safest repellent yet!

*Ultrasonic electronic bug eradicators.* Remember those small ultrasonic electronic devices that gave off a sound that supposedly repelled mosquitoes? They didn't prove to be worth anything, but you might want to do your part for the betterment of science and experiment with your vibrator. You could investigate which of the variable speeds of your vibrator is most effective at warding off mosquitoes.

*Permethrin.* The most effective is . . . Permethrin is a powerful and rapidly acting, human-made synthetic insecticide that was originally derived from the chrysanthemum flower. It does not repel insects but works as a contact insecticide, knocking the little suckers right out of the air. It is effective against mosquitoes, flies, ticks, and chiggers. Permethrin, found in a spray called Repel Permanone Tick Repellent, has low toxicity in mammals (that's you) and is poorly absorbed by the skin.

Permethrin should be applied directly to clothing (two

hours before putting it on) or other fabrics (such as tent walls or mosquito nets), not to skin. It lasts at least two weeks. Permethrin-treated clothing plus skin application of a medium DEET-based repellent seems to be the most effective combination against mosquito and other bug bites.

*Mosquito jacket.* The Mississauga Mosquito Jacket is made of netting that keeps out black flies and mosquitoes. The hood has a piece that can zipper over the face. It fits loosely over your clothes, with cuffs at the wrists and waist. Matching pants are also available.

*Mosquito nets.* Mosquito nets come in various shapes, from rectangular to tent shaped. One in the Campmor catalog looks like it could house a small harem. It's called a Traveller's Mosquito Net, and it hangs from one suspension point, spread over a double-bed-size area.

*Or go to bed early.* This may seem like a sacrifice, but once you're in the tent, I'm sure you will find ways to amuse yourselves.

### Treatments

If those little creatures do bite you, a number of products on the market will ease the itch.

*Benadryl.* Benadryl is available in a clear antihistamine gel and relieves itches from insect bites and poison ivy, oak, and sumac.

*Topical corticosteroids.* These are probably the most effective in reducing the redness and itching.

*Clearly Cala Anti-Itch Medicated Gel.* Clearly Cala Anti-Itch Medicated Gel serves as a skin protectant, antihistamine, and anaesthetic. It relieves the itching and pain of insect bites and other general discomforts like poison oak and ivy, skin allergies, rashes, minor burns, and minor skin irritations.

*The ultimate relief.* Get away from the little bastards.

## WHAT MAKES ITCH?

Typically the itch from a bug bite or poisonous plant is a mild local allergic reaction. The bug or plant sticks you with a poison, and your body reacts. Among the reactions is the release of histamines, a compound found in all cells, which in turn causes itching. Antihistamines (like Benadryl) block histamine receptors, so the histamines will no longer cause itching.

## "ASS-PRIN" PASTE

If you get a bug bite in any very inappropriate place, you probably don't want to put chemicals on it. But you don't want it to itch either. (We're talking about the private parts here.) One folk remedy that seems to work remarkably well is aspirin. No, don't eat it—smash it up, make a paste, and press it onto (or into, as the case may be) the bite. Swelling, itching, and redness disappear instantly, and you can resume your activities.

# Chapter 8

## ANIMAL MAGNETISM

*"Always look out for Number One and be careful not to step in Number Two."*

—RODNEY DANGERFIELD

**A**nimals live in the woods. It's their home. Sighting various wild animals may add ambience and intrigue to your outing, and with a little preplanning you can avoid mishaps and protect yourselves from unwanted disturbances. Believe me, it will be worth it.

For the most part, keep your eyes open, and don't approach wild animals. The little critters can be more worrisome than the big guys, most of the time anyway. Chipmunks bite, raccoons raid your garbage, and camp robbers (birds) are called that for a reason. If you find any creatures are trying to horn in on your fun, here are a few suggestions for dealing with them.

A lot of the rules for humans and romance apply to other animals as well. The more you know about animals, the less fearful you'll be and the more fulfilling your experiences.

# The Bear Necessities: How to Outrun a Bear with Your Pants Around Your Ankles

The good news is you don't have to outrun a bear with your pants around your ankles, because running is seldom the most effective means of escaping from or deterring a wild animal.

Oscar and Lucinda were hiking in the hills of Montana last summer. It was just a day hike, although Oscar was fully prepared for "nightlike" activities. He had his blanket, condoms, and water bottle—he was one prepared dude, or so he thought. As they crossed an avalanche chute, Lucinda realized they were in territory that might attract black bears. She warned Oscar, and they started talking a little louder to announce their existence to any possible nearby bears.

As they ambled along arm in arm, they noticed a huge black bear sniffing the air they had just stirred. Oscar was ready to run for the hills, but Lucinda kept her cool and clutched Oscar to keep him in place. Can't outrun a bear, you know. Poor Oscar. Not much cools an amorous foreplay stroll better than the threat of being eaten by a bear.

Fortunately, our happy couple did all the right things. First, they recognized that the avalanche chute—with its grasses, forbs, and berries—was prime black bear country. Another sign is mauled logs, overturned rocks, and damaged trees. And if you are so inquisitive as to turn over a pile of scat and find green vegetation, look out! If the scat is still steaming, you know a bear is really close.

Look for fresh bear tracks. They look a lot like humans', with five toes front and back—except that humans usually wear boots up in the mountains. Tiny tracks indicate a bear cub alert. And you certainly don't want to come between a mom and her cubs.

Our happy couple also made noise. Spooking a bear is never a good idea—a startled bear is likely to rear up, hiss, and breathe out with a snort. (Heavy breathing is a reaction you'd rather encounter during your intimate afternoon recreation.) Our educated couple backed away slowly and tried to look bigger than they were (not easy when you're frightened and want to look invisible).

If you do encounter a black bear, don't scream or wave your arms. Don't stare the bear down, and don't imitate any aggressive sounds the bear might adopt. If it barks or lays its ears back, it's about to charge. Drop something, like a pack, to distract it, and back away. If it charges, stand your ground and fight back with sticks, rocks, your feet—anything! Don't play dead, as you would with a grizzly.

Our ever-so-prepared Lucinda just happened to have a can of Counter Assault. She pulled it out and had it poised and ready for action. Counter Assault is a spray of capsicum and cayenne pepper. It irritates the assailant's eyes, nose, and throat, without doing permanent damage. Fortunately, they were able to back away safely. The bear meandered off toward a pile of berries, leaving our friends shaken but unharmed. As they continued their hike, all Oscar could think about was that can of Counter Assault. Had Lucinda brought it to protect him or to use on him?

## Food Hang-Ups

Did you know you can get arrested for keeping a cooler on the picnic table? Unbeknownst to Andy and Kathleen, Forest Service rangers are officers of the law and can ticket or arrest you for just such an offense. Not only did our happy couple not hang up their food bag, they had the audacity to leave a cooler on the table for any neighbors or critters to help themselves for a midnight snack.

In the bright morning sunlight, Andy and Kathleen emerged from their tent all rosy and cozy to find not only a ticket on their cooler but a forest ranger approaching them, looking most unpleased. In many public camping facilities bears and other animals apparently have become so conditioned that the sight (even without a smell) of a cooler triggers the "food" response, and they help themselves.

Embarrassed by their disheveled appearance and lack of much in the way of clothing, the ranger bade them a good morning and mumbled, "I'll let this be a warning to you, but just this time."

## Bear-Bagging

Especially in populated camping areas, bears have developed quite a discriminating palate for just the kinds of food people like to bring on camping trips. I would be remiss to omit it from this text, since a bear disturbance could really be a nuisance.

Store all food and related supplies in metal storage boxes, where provided. If you are car camping, stick it in your trunk. Store out of sight and smell all grocery bags, garbage, and scented articles, such as soap, sunscreen, hairspray, Chapstick, lip gloss, lipstick, and toothpaste.

Sorry to say, bear-bagging is not as kinky as it sounds. (That would be "bare-bagging"—and I'm not sure what activity that word conjures up.) Bear-bagging is a method of keeping the bear population from rifling through your food, clamoring around your campsite, and more importantly, from disturbing you while you are engaged in far more important matters in your tent.

Counterbalanced bear-bagging is simply suspending your food at one end of a rope and hanging another weight (which may also be food) at the other end. To bear-bag: Tie a rock or heavy object to the end of a fifty-plus-foot parachute cord, and toss it over a branch. Think of it as lassoing a branch with a fifty-foot rope. It's easier than a bull or steer, because the branch isn't moving.

Remove the rock, and tie on a heavier stuff sack. Hoist

the stuff sack up to the branch, and tie the other weight to the cord you are holding. Tie it as high as possible. Put the leftover cord in the sack except for the end, which should be made into a loop.

Push the lighter sack up with a stick. Push until the sacks are at the same height, twelve feet off ground. One sack must be heavier for gravity to work for you.

To retrieve the sack, snag the loop with a stick, and pull it down. The sacks should be ten feet from the tree trunk, five feet from the top of branch, and twelve feet from the ground. You probably didn't bring a tape measure, so you're going to have to wing it and fling it.

In bear country, since you can't bear-bag yourselves (I knew we'd get a little kinky), keep your odiferous intimate paraphernalia at a minimum. Use odorless creams and lubricants, and Ziploc all refuse. And remember, bears are attracted to the smell of blood, so no biting!

*Warning:* If you are menstruating in heavily populated carnivore country, use tampons, not pads. Burn or Ziploc all refuse. Hang refuse with the food (in an "appropriate container," of course). Don't bury it or toss it into a latrine.

In all seriousness, it's best to pack out tampons and used sex refuse. The odor from them (either the perfume before or the other odors after) may attract bears or other animals. If you bury them, they'll just be dug up. While in camp, it's best to keep them safely away from the tent and out of reach and to *take them out* when you leave. Again, while menstruation is not a proven bear problem, it isn't in the clear, either.

And, hey—some people pack toilet paper out. Yes, used toilet paper. I've done that several times myself, but I generally bury it with what we'll call "the product"—mixing it in well with a stick so it doesn't cause a litter problem. That's all I'm going to say about *that*. Again, burn or Ziploc all refuse. Don't bury it or toss it in a latrine.

## Burning the Evidence

One evening Sean, a backcountry ranger, saw a fire off in the distance. Since this was a "no forest fire" facility, it was his responsibility to contact those engaging in pyro delights. The next morning he located a guy drinking coffee near an obviously extinguished campfire. When reminded of the no-burn policy, the guy responded that he was burning used tampons to destroy their odor, so as not to entice any bears or other such blood-seeking creatures. It was hard for Sean to argue with that logic.

(The guy seemed like he was alone. As Sean walked away, he wondered whose they were.)

## Grizzlies

*"My advice for grizzlies is to try to maintain sphincter control!"*
—KERRY SNOW, *volunteer trail manager with the Potomac Appalachian Trail Club (PATC)*

According to Dean Ahearn, outdoorsman and bear aficionado for PATC, if you're headed to Glacier Park in Alaska, grizzlies should be high on your plan-ahead list. Going into country where they're prevalent requires a bit of preparation and forethought. (Ditto for going into black bear country that almost never sees human visitation, by the way.) Bears in the lower forty-eight states have learned about us and take greater pains to avoid us. But in some places, remote places, such as in northern Canada and Alaska, a black bear's first thought might be, "Large protein source." Probably won't be, but might be. Do your homework in these situations.

# Other Animals

When you are out in the woods, there are a few general animal rules to consider. Running is virtually never advisable, unless you want to be chased. Not exclusively a human response, running can trigger a predatory or aggressive response in any animal so inclined. All such animals can outrun you, and most wouldn't have been interested in attacking you to begin with had you not fled.

The lone exception to this might be a swarm of angry bees or other stinging insects. Run like hell—and head for deep water or enclosed shelter if available. Otherwise, keep running. With killer bees, you might have to run a long way. Run!

Another bad idea is "staring down." Most animals our size or bigger, carnivore and herbivore alike, take a stare as a challenge and may respond appropriately. (Dogs, too.) Even when standing your ground and looking as threatening as possible is the thing to do, as in a face-to-face confrontation with a mountain lion, for instance (lucky you!), prolonged eye-to-eye is inadvisable. Obviously, don't take your eye off the animal; that could be *really* dangerous. But don't measure its eyeballs, either. Just "keep track of it."

### Mountain Lions

*Mountain lion, cougar, puma, catamount,* and *panther* are all names for the same animal. They are elusive and reclusive, and sightings are rare. They aren't particularly interested in humans, but remember, they are higher up on the food chain than you. They are very fast runners—don't try to outrun them. After you've taken a good look at one, which is a rare treat, clamor and make a lot of noise so you don't startle it. Not to hurt your ego, but they're usually not particularly interested in you.

## Cougar Cub Alarm Clock

Nancy and Jamie were driving along the beautiful Oregon coast hunting in vain for a campground. Finally they decided to pull their vehicle off the road and lay their tarp on a field. They then spread out their sleeping bags and folded the other half of the tarp over themselves. As they frolicked, they felt like mincemeat in a tarp sandwich.

Later Nancy awoke to loud purring. As she opened her eyes, she was face-to-face with a cougar cub that was staring curiously down at her. Off in the distance she heard a loud, much lower purr. Mother Cougar was summoning her baby away. Nancy tried to lie very quietly. After a vain attempt to return to sleep, she decided it was time to get up and go in search of a Starbucks for their morning latte. (This was the West Coast, after all.)

## Skunks

It's not the big dangerous creatures that you're most likely to have trouble with—it's the pesky smaller ones that steal your food, bite your cords, or just smell bad.

Let's take the "smell bad" critter, for example. Kerry Snow, volunteer trail manager with PATC, was innocently sleeping, minding his own business after a day of back-packing in Shenandoah National Park. In the middle of the night, he awoke and immediately got this sinking feeling in his chest. It's a good thing he awoke calmly, because right there sitting on his chest was a skunk. (No wonder he had a sinking feeling.) Kerry moved and twisted ever so slightly, just enough to jostle the black and white creature but not enough to really disturb it. The skunk slid off the sleeping bag, waddled away, and disappeared into the trees.

The general rule when meeting a skunk is to back *slowly* away or past the fellow. If one visits your campsite, be still and let it eat whatever it damn well pleases. It will eventually tire of you and go elsewhere.

## Elk

Elk travel in herds. Which means they also shit in herds. Maybe nature calls them all at the same time, or maybe seeing one elk eliminate stimulates the others to do the same. Ian and Joyce came upon one such "dumping ground." A sunny clearing over a rise had beckoned them. As they approached it, they pulled out their blanket in preparation for a little fun in the sun. But in their bliss they hadn't paid attention to the "barnyard step" they had just performed. They looked around to see that they were literally in the midst of *acres* of elk shit, evenly distributed about one pile per square foot.

## Bats

Humans aren't the only ones who do their most important activities at night. Bats, too, come to life as the sun goes down. At dusk, if you see the darting and jutting of what looks like low-flying birds, they are probably bats. Bats don't get tangled in your hair, and they are no more likely to carry rabies than any other wild animal. And only two or three of the thousand bat species are vampire bats, which lick (not suck) blood from farm animals in Central and South America.

If bats are around, consider yourself fortunate. Little brown bats (the ones you're most likely to see) only weigh a quarter-ounce, but they can eat more than a thousand mosquitoes and other bugs in a night. The mama bat holds the record. While nursing, she'll eat up to six hundred mosquitoes an hour for four to six hours. That's about three thousand insects (nearly twice her weight). Bats dine on the very insects that can ruin, or at least interfere with, your whole evening. Thanks, bats.

### Snakes

Snakes? Watch where you step! Go well around them or avoid them altogether. In the United States you'd have to almost try to get bitten. When you are in snake country, your best defenses are to watch where you're reaching and stepping, wear high-top boots, and step on top of obstructions rather than over them.

If you happen to be bitten, keep the punctured area below heart level, and remain calm. Exert yourself as little as possible. This is your chance to let someone else take care of you for a while. If you can get out of the woods quickly, do so. But if you can't, remember that snakebites are almost never fatal in North America. You'll probably be pretty miserable for a while, but you'll live.

A device called the Extractor can be used to suck out venom without making an incision. I'm not recommending you use this or any snakebite kit, but if you are planning on carrying one, *know how to use it before you take it out.* Practice at home. Make sure you know what everything in the kit is and does. And play-act with the kit—you know, sort of like playing doctor when you were a kid.

The tourniquet is a dangerous and controversial first-aid technique. It is used only when the only other choice is certain death. When a tourniquet is applied above the bite, it helps prevent the poison from flowing through the body. But it also stops fresh blood from flowing to that limb, and the limb could be lost. The old cut-and-suck method is not really advised either anymore, as you could suck the poison into your own mouth.

According to John Ketchum (Trails Forum, PATC):

*I am not unacquainted with the dangers of snake encounters. Once I came too close for comfort. Having broken my brand-new fly rod the night before, I was sitting on a rock above the creek reading and sipping wine instead of fishing. I rose and walked over to camp for a wine refill. On returning, I looked for a spot to set my cup before plopping my glutei maximi onto the rock. Good thing, because where I had been sitting less than five minutes before, and where I was about to sit, was a three-foot copperhead, staring at me. I decided to sit elsewhere.*

*As I gradually awoke the next morning, I felt something cold move against my leg in my sleeping bag. I lay there, unmoving, while something about the size of a snakehead kept nudging my foot. When my bladder could stand it no longer, I made the fastest exit ever from sleeping bag and tent. When I gingerly dumped the bag, out fell a small toad that had apparently snuck into the tent while I was arranging gear.*

---

### S n a k e b i t e

Don't take this as an antidote, but if you've just had a bad scare, one of these may help you relax:

1¼ oz. Yukon Jack
¾ oz. Triple Sec
Lime juice

1. Combine all ingredients.
2. Chill and strain into a cocktail glass

## Bootlicking Bunny

It was a gorgeous star-studded summer night high up in the Pasayten Wilderness. The thought of making love seemed delightful, but for wild and woolly Waldo and Jazmyne, the inside of a tent would have been far too confining. They set up a tarp, laid out their sleeping bags, and began "discovering" each other under the stars. They had just stopped for a breather and were staring up at the sky when they heard little scratches and licks about three feet from their heads. Realizing it wasn't each other, the sweaty couple reached for illumination. Beaming the flashlight in its eyes, they saw they were being coached by a bootlicking bunny, who thought he'd get into a little kink action, too. How'd the bunny know this couple was into that kind of stuff?

After you've read all this, remember: Your chances of getting into a truly dangerous situation with a large wild animal are pretty slim. Read up a bit before you go, stay alert, and you shouldn't have a problem.

As with love, there are no guarantees. And I hope there never are.

# Chapter 9

---

## SEX GAMES TO PLAY IN THE WOODS

*"If I could sleep I might make love. I'd go into the woods. My eyes would see . . . the sky, the earth. I'd run, run, they wouldn't catch me."*

—SAMUEL BECKETT

## Games Introduction

Do you know the rule about "in bed" for fortune cookies? When you get those ridiculous fortune cookies—which, of course, have very personal and pertinent fortunes—you do take them seriously, don't you? Well, if you don't believe "This month will bring you great joy" or "You will meet someone who will change your life," you can at least add a little humor to this otherwise paltry excuse for dessert (or for fortune, for that matter). Just add "in bed" to the end of your fortune and put a smile on your face. "Your hard work will pay off soon . . . in bed." "Many appreciate your generosity . . . in bed." "If your desires are not extravagant, they will be granted—in bed."

Now, what do fortune cookies have to do with sex games in the woods? As with the fortune cookie, just alter the rules of almost any regular game a little bit, and you can make it a sex game.

# Group Games

## Sexual Pictionary

We'll start with Sexual Pictionary. Regular Pictionary is the ever-so-popular game that challenges not only your artistic ability but your imagination, as well as your word-association and quick-thinking abilities. Remember the basic rules? Your partner draws a picture, and you have one minute to guess what it is.

Just like adding "in bed" to fortune cookies, with Sexual Pictionary all the words or phrases are sex-related. This is a great group after-dinner game.

*Equipment.* Out in the woods you probably won't have several pads of paper, pencils, a table, and good lighting— all equipment we take for granted in our living rooms. So as with everything else you do in the woods, you improvise. You can play Sexual Pictionary on a smoothed section of sand or dirt. And you draw the pictures with a stick. A stopwatch or a watch with a second hand may be helpful.

*The object.* To have fun drawing dirty pictures in the sand and laughing with your friends.

*Preparation.* If you're planning a camping trip with a group of lighthearted perverts, you might want to make up cards ahead of time.

- Divide the group into two teams.
- Each team selects a Picturist for the first round.
- Select one person to be the designated Whisperer. The Whisperer can use a word or phrase from the list on the next page or make up one, which the two Picturists will draw.
- Clear a large area of dirt or sand. Divide it in half, so that each team has a drawing board.

***Rules.***

- The Whisperer selects a card and shows it only to the two Picturists.
- On "go," the two Picturists draw. They can't use verbal cues or physical communication. As the Picturists draw, each team tries to guess what word or phrase the Picturists are drawing. They shout out possible answers for their own Picturist.
- The first team to guess correctly gets a point.
- If no one guesses within the time limit (like a minute), no score is received.
- If you want to keep score, mark notches in the dirt.
- Each team then selects a new Picturist, and they go for round two.
- The game ends when it gets too dark to see, or when one team reaches a predetermined score, or when you feel like quitting.

***Suggested topics.*** Here is the list of suggested topics for the Whisperer. You can make up cards ahead of time:

- Headache
- Vasectomy
- Vagina
- Penis
- Lingerie
- Missionary position
- Vibrator
- Blue balls
- Blind date
- Oral sex
- Abstinence
- Viagra

- Nymphomaniac
- Orgy
- PMS
- Masturbation
- Hickey
- French kiss
- Orgasm
- Crotchless panties

## The Chair Game

When you were in elementary school, you may have played Musical Chairs at a birthday party. The chair game is similar, in that there will always be one chair less than the number of people playing.

How many people in your group have sex secrets or experiences that are unknown to the rest of the group? I bet you everyone has done something in his or her own sordid past that he or she considers unique or different from what others have done. Well, it's time to clean out those closets and play the Chair Game!

The Chair Game is a rather innocent title for a revealing game. It is a "Have you ever————?" or "How many have ever————?" kind of game.

*Rules.* Make a circle of chairs or other items to sit on. Since you are in the woods, you are likely to end up with a combination of Crazy Creek seats, Therm-a-Rest pads, Insulite pads, blankets, and even jackets. They can be anything you can rest your butt on in a hurry. Be sure there is one less "sit-upon" than there are people playing.

The person in the middle is It. It asks, "How many have ever————?" then proceeds to fill in the blank with something that is true for her or him. That's important! For the person who is It, the answer to the question must be yes.

*Movement.* All of the participants for whom the statement

is true must stand up and find another chair. It also finds a chair. Now, if this is a big math problem for you, you're not old enough to be reading this book. But as you have figured out by now, there will always be some poor sucker without a chair. Yep, you guessed it—that chairless wonder becomes the next It. He or she has to come up with the next embarrassing, strut-your-stuff, or tell-all question. This game could (and has) gone on for several hours, since no one ever loses (except maybe their secrets).

*Question suggestions.* The following is a list of Chair Game starter questions. I have witnessed them with my very own ears. (For the record, they are not necessarily from my own experience.)

They should all be prefaced with the words "How many have ever———?"

- Made love outdoors
- Had someone walk in on you while making love
- Masturbated with a foreign object (or a domestic object for that matter)
- Been in a *ménage à trois*
- Gone skinny-dipping
- Been involved with oral sex in a moving vehicle
- Given or gotten a hickey
- While having sex, thought about a different person than the one you were with
- Worn underwear you'd be embarrassed to have others see
- Had sex with someone whose name you didn't know
- Faked an orgasm
- Been tied up during sex
- Made love with a person of your own gender
- Had an affair with a married person
- Farted during lovemaking

***Fessing up.*** Obviously, admitting to some of these things could be very incriminating or even downright lethal. The items on this list run the gamut from being funny and embarrassing to being potentially damaging.

I don't need to tell you that this is only a game. Therefore it is wise to begin by stating: "If you are playing this game, and there is a secret you aren't ready to tell, or a situation that would be all out stupid for you to admit—keep your mouth shut and stay seated in the chair!" If no one knows what you're not admitting, they still aren't going to know if you don't stand up!

## Therm-a-Rest Butt Prints

A group of health educators used a rafting trip as the setting for a conference. They decided to make it a "clothing optional" excursion. River rafting? Clothing optional? There was barely a stitch in sight. Amidst the rafting, the group's focus was on such topics as group dynamics, process, and communication. One day they were all having a meeting in the hot sun, processing everything from "jokes appropriate to tell in the workplace" to "surviving menopause." After baking for at least an hour, they got up for a break. Catherine noticed that the sweat from her exposed bottom had created a rather interesting shape on her now-sweaty Therm-a-Rest pad. Joe came over, laughing: "Your butt print looks like one of those inkblot tests." It was near-perfectly symmetrical and looked like a butterfly.

"No," chimed Ethel, "that print is trying to tell us that Catherine is a free-thinking spirit. Look at the way the shape flows." Well, this group wasn't about to let this idea go unexploited, so they started looking at the other pads. Each had a sweaty (and probably smelly) individualized butt print. The group then proceeded to analyze each print and identify what it said about its owner. Things like:

- Broad in the beam
- Anally retentive
- "This multilayered print is obviously from some antsy person who can't sit still."
- The densest, clearest print was from the person who seemed most settled in life.
- "Must be very lazy—no shape whatsoever!"
- Happy-go-lucky, paranoid, frivolous, intellectual, a gourmet cook, orderly, efficient, and so forth

What would *your* butt print look like?

***Make your own butt print.*** This could be a great way to get your partner to hang out naked in the hot sunshine. Tell him or her that you have to see if you have compatible butt prints. Of course you run the risk of coming off as a total lunatic, but maybe that's part of your charm!

**I Always Wanted to Know . . .**

This one's a couples' game. All the players write down on a piece of paper a question they've always wanted to know about their partner's sexual desires. These are then folded and put in a hat. The hat is passed around the circle, and each person draws out one question, reads it aloud, and answers it as honestly as possible. Although you won't necessarily get to know what your own partner would say, you sure do get a broad perspective on what others think and do. This could certainly lead to some interesting discussions on the trail the next day.

# Games for Two

**Sexual Roulette**

Sounds dangerous? Well, brace yourself. No blanks will be shot in this loaded game of chance and erotic maneuvers.

Get ready for some good clean one-on-one fun in the sun (or moonlight).

I got the idea for this game from a twenty-four-sided sphere called Le Carouselle that somehow made its way into my dresser and took up permanent residence there.

For this game, you'll want to select a playmate who is limber and not too squeamish about receiving or giving upon command. You simply roll the sphere and perform the assigned task.

*Rules.* Since it is unlikely that you have a twenty-four-sided sphere on your camping list, I've come up with some alternatives.

Four dice could easily solve the problem. When it's your turn, simply pick up any number of dice and toss them. Add up the numbers on the faces of the dice. Then read the corresponding item on the following list. Since you are at the mercy of your dice roll, you must now do as the number dictates (or negotiate for a new roll).

No dice? Write the numbers 1 to 24 on little slips of paper and fold them. Instead of rolling dice, each person picks a slip and does as the number dictates.

Since this is your list, you may replace any seen item on it with something else that's titillating. I've never written instructions for this game, so there's no formal way to end it. I guess you could say, "It ain't over till it's over."

1. Give your partner a slow cheek-to-cheek hug and kiss.
2. Lean over the woman while she is on her hands and knees.
3. Kiss your lover behind the ears and neck for two minutes.
4. Kiss your partner's chosen erotic spot.
5. French-kiss your partner for five minutes.
6. Sit on your partner's lap face-to-face, and rock back and forth for two minutes (no intercourse).
7. Give your lover a sexy compliment.

8. Take the 69 position with your partner.
9. Lick and gently suck on your lover's nipples.
10. Put jam on your partner's belly and lick it off.
11. Caress your lover's belly, hips, and thighs.
12. Have the woman sit on top, facing or reversed.
13. Sit on your partner's belly with the weight on your own legs, and rock gently.
14. Dance naked together.
15. Find a leaf, feather, or grasses, and gently tickle your partner while lying down.
16. Gently kiss and nibble on your lover's hips and thighs.
17. Give your lover a back massage.
18. Tell your partner a sex fantasy.
19. Suck on your partner's fingers one by one.
20. Lick your lover's palms.
21. Give your partner a five-minute massage.
22. Perform a strip-tease dance for your partner.
23. Suck on your partner's toes one at a time.
24. Run your fingers through your lover's hair.

Try not to let yourselves come to orgasm during the above, or the game may be over prematurely.

## Strip Sticks

You may not have a deck of cards out in the woods, or the inclination to actually play poker, but you can always play Sticks. Sticks is a very simple game with absolutely no strategy. It simply calls for two sticks—a short one and a little shorter one. One person holds the two sticks, concealing their length. The other person picks one. The one who ends up with the shorter stick has to remove an article of clothing. Oh, did I forget to mention this game is like Strip Poker? This part of the game is the "strip"; the "poker" part comes later in the tent.

David played this game when he was ten years old. It was

his first memory of titillation. He and eleven-year-old Heather were on an annual family camping trip. They went off to play and explore the woods—or so he thought. When they stopped to rest, Heather suggested they play Sticks. She told David the rules. He didn't know what to make of the whole thing, but it sounded pretty good to him.

They started to play, first removing a sneaker, then a sock, then a sweatshirt. Soon things started getting a little cheek-blushingly close to the underwear layer.

David couldn't chicken out, but he didn't know what he'd do if things progressed further. But before the underwear sticks were drawn, they heard their names being called in the distance. Phew! Saved by the bell. They scurried to put their clothes back on and trotted back to the campsite. For the whole rest of the camping trip, David could think of nothing but the next stick being drawn. Just as the families were loading the cars, Heather leaned over and whispered in his ear, "We'll play that game again next year." Her remark remains emblazoned in his memory to this day.

## Progressive Sex Day Hike

Have you ever attended one of those progressive dinners where each person prepares a course of the meal, and you go from house to house enjoying an extended meal with friends? How about progressive sex? I'm not suggesting this as a group activity (although that would be up to you and your friends). These are suggestions for a two-person interlude—asking any additional invitees is entirely your prerogative.

You and your partner are on a day hike up a lightly populated trail. In this game each of you is responsible for special foreplay activities. At each rest stop along the trail, you take turns leading an activity (or lesson, as the case may be). The scenario might go as follows:

*Stop one.* Hike about fifteen minutes. It's your turn. You

give your partner a big sensuous kiss and a few nibbles on the neck. You run your fingers under his or her shirt, up the bare back, and down onto those soft warm buns.

*Stop two.* After hiking for another twenty minutes, your partner leads you behind a tree and pulls you into his or her body, caressing your outer thighs. Gentle fingertips work their way up the leg of your shorts and gently rub the warm soft skin just inside.

*Stop three.* It must be time for a snack by now. Tell your partner to sit down and that your hands alone will do the feeding. He or she sits down against a tree as you pull out a bunch of grapes. You straddle those strong thighs and hold the grapes up just out of reach, so he or she has to flex both thigh muscles under your warm bottom to reach nourishment. Then you offer a few more grapes by placing them between your teeth and passing them to moist awaiting lips.

*Stop four.* For the next course, your partner removes your shirt, takes a dollop of cream cheese, smears it onto one of your nipples, and cleans it completely, leaving no traces.

You get my drift. I don't have to put words on your lips or guide your hands. I'm sure you can figure it out. Continue your hike, taking turns, until you find a pleasant, secluded, sunny spot to enjoy the main course of this Progressive Sex Hike.

## Sex Toys: Natural and Human-Made

The woods provide a natural setting in which fantasies can take on a life of their own. When you're away from the confines of your four walls and your daily life, your imagination may begin to wander. Look around for natural objects that can serve as toys to heighten your outdoor sexual experience. With a little creativity, feathers, smooth rocks, soft flowers, water, and tree bark all have erotic potential.

Susan was a medical-school model. Her job was to be

poked and prodded, laid out, and bandaged by budding young medical students. On this particular Monday morning, the class was practicing gynecological techniques. Susan nonchalantly lay down on the table and placed her feet in those freezing-cold stirrups. Sam, who was admittedly a little nervous, donned his latex gloves and lubed them properly with K-Y jelly. He gently placed one hand on Susan's belly and inserted his two fingers inside her. It's hard to say who was more surprised when Sam pulled not one but two smooth, round rocks from her vagina.

Apparently while on their weekend camping trip, Susan and her husband, Fred, had used little stones from a rushing stream as *ben wa* balls. She thought he had removed them but was embarrassingly mistaken come Monday morning.

### *Ben Wa* Balls

Three quarters to one and a half inches in size, *ben wa* balls are metal balls that are inserted into the vagina to heighten sexual sensation. Their legend and mystique have been carried down from ancient Japanese women, who apparently inserted two hollow ivory balls filled with mercury into their vaginas and sat back to enjoy the sensation. (I hope the poisonous liquid was just part of a legend, or else those women were in real trouble.)

Today *ben wa* balls can be used as a solo performance, in which a woman inserts them and goes about her day. But how does this differ from a tampon? Maybe just knowing they're in there is the turn-on. Hey, maybe to some, a tampon is an erotic sex toy. Some claim that the presence of *ben wa* balls during intercourse provides added sensation, but here too the balls have received little actual acclaim. They seem to be somewhat overrated.

In any case, if they turn you on, *ben wa* river rocks may add to your au natural experience.

**Feathers**

*"Kinky sex involves the use of duck feathers. Perverted sex involves the whole duck."*

—LEWIS GIZZARD

Your skin is the largest sense organ on your body. Millions of nerve endings are distributed in various concentrations, not just on your genitals and designated erogenous zones, but all over you. Lightly touching one's skin often brings goose bumps to the surface. Fingertips dancing on the skin do a fine job of arousing that tingling sensation. But no matter how lightly they tickle, fingers aren't as delicate as the touch of a feather. You can either purchase feathers before your camping excursion or look for them on the trail.

Be warned: If you use feathers from the wild, double-check for bugs nestled in the base of the feather shaft. Spray the feathers with rubbing alcohol to thwart any residual creatures left from the host bird.

***Light as a feather.*** Have your partner lie face-up naked, with eyes closed. Hmm, that sounds like a good start for just about anything. . . . Oh yeah, the feathers. Without giving any warning of where this bird will land next, lightly touch down and stroke along the inside of the arm, the sole of the foot, the side of the neck. Bask your lover in a delightful feather bath.

# Bondage

The cardinal bondage rule—"Never leave unattended someone who's tied up"—goes double in the woods. You'd never want your partner to be at the mercy of some fellow camper or creepy crawler.

If you are using ropes or scarves, don't use thin or slippery ones—they may tighten or be hard to untie. You may remember from your knot-tying days that bowlines work well, while slipknots can tighten in an untimely manner. Since outdoors you are more vulnerable, you and your partner may want to keep the knots loose enough to slip out of easily. The power is the play. If your imagination tells you that you are bound and at the mercy of your partner, then there's no escape!

## Harness the Power

Even the hardest-core climber must sometimes look at those climbing harnesses with some degree of lust in mind. All they need is the "strap-on tool," and they are ready for action! If you already have a harness, it may be fun to wear it bare-bottomed as a sexual bondage toy. Or attach a vibrator or dildo to this contraption, with a belt or extra webbing to carry out various erotic fantasies.

If you aren't a climber but would like to give this activity a shot, try it! Out in the woods is a great place to pull out the stops, so to speak. Harnesses offer different features for different functions:

- Arborists (tree workers) get strapped in and climb trees with chain saws in hand. Some older arborist saddles are simply buttstraps that run from hip to hip, clamping the thighs together— obviously dysfunctional for the likes of this book.
- The recreational rock climber's goal is to get from the bottom to the top and back using mostly body strength but having a safe, strong backup support. Rock climbers use a lightly padded webbing that cuts into the leg, affectionately known as the "crotch-killer saddle." Since their ethic is not to rely on the rope, they apparently don't want the harness to be too comfortable.

- Kinky sex partners hang around playing the S&M game and require easy access to key areas. S&M harnesses were designed for kink over comfort. The thin leather or vinyl straps will hold you for a while but definitely don't make you feel at home.

Specialty stores, along with mail-order and website catalogs, offer reasonable quality and variety in harnesses. Adult bookstores seem to stock cheaper, less functional models. When shopping for a harness, look closely at how it adjusts, how it will fit, what it exposes, and what it covers. For example, if you're not into that butt-floss feel, take note of where the straps line up. (See Resources.)

**Harness Happiness (Tree Swing)**

Having reviewed the choices, I'd say the Ness Saddle (from New Tribe) is by far the best sex harness for hanging barebottomed in a tree and having saddle sex. With its large padded leg support, no webbing or fabric will cut into your naked butt. It's like hanging in a self-contained swing. And since you will be totally accessible, your partner can tease you, sit on you, or have his or her way with you in whatever manner seems appropriate. You could even get two Ness Saddles and swing together, wrap your legs around each other, and so on—but make sure you find a good sturdy tree.

# Games for One: You Are Your Own Best Friend

Let's face it, the woods make lots of people horny. But not everyone always has the luxury of a ready and willing, mutually consenting adult partner. The fullness of the solitude of solo camping can also include experiencing total pleasure with no inhibitions, no encumbrances, and no other being to consider.

In other words, sometimes we have to take matters into our own hands.

### Aqua Vulva

Here's an interesting product that will definitely make you "master of your domain."

Men, add Aqua Vulva to your list of camping essentials. It's the first men's sex toy to use water to adjust temperature and fit. Fill the three separate baffles, then brace it with pillows or use it manually to create your own virtual-sex experience.

Resembling a child's floatation sleeve, the twenty-four-inch Aqua Vulva consists of three plastic channels that can be filled with air, water, or any combination thereof. Each sleeve has a water valve and an air valve, so you can regulate the water-versus-air-pressure ratio for use as a limb brace, a hot/cold water bottle, or—you guessed it—a water-filled vagina.

# Chapter 10

---

## THE LAW

> *"The laws sometimes sleep, but never die."*
> —INSCRIPTION ON A FORTUNE COOKIE

A lot of sex in the woods goes unnoticed, seldom seen, and certainly unchastised. This is the kind among four-legged creatures and others who inhabit the woods. If you happen to see this sort of interaction, consider yourself lucky. This favorable attitude, however, does not prevail when two-legged humans engage in such animal behavior. For the most part, people would rather not come upon two humans having sex in the woods. But is it illegal? That is the question we are dealing with in this chapter.

## Prudent Old Laws and Semi-enforceable Current Laws

Many people assume that if they are caught having sex in an exposed outdoor area, they could get into serious legal trouble. For others, their sense of moral conduct helps them maintain at least a level of discretion.

What actually can and can't you do, to and with whom,

and where and when? Finding out is not a task for the faint of heart. I interviewed park rangers, police officers, lawyers, and judges. I even searched the new all-knowing authority, the Internet. One lawyer, between giving me laws, court cases, and his noble opinion, found himself calculating the number of times he himself had had sex in the woods. He proudly reached his final tally. I didn't let on how unimpressed I was by the number, but I did suggest he get back out there and rekindle his youth. As he let himself take a stroll down memory lane, he wistfully added, "I hope every adult has had sex in the woods at least once." We wholeheartedly agreed there is something magical about making love in the great outdoors.

Finally I came up with some clarity about the legalities. To immediately put your mind at ease, no laws on any books specifically state that sex in the woods is illegal. This would be a really short chapter and end right here, except that there are also a few notable details that I would be remiss if I did not share with you.

## The Blanket Statement

When I asked another lawyer about the legalities of having sex in the woods, his immediate response was "Bring a blanket." Covering up is apparently the important factor here. It's something like the ostrich with its head in the sand: If they can't tell what you're doing, you can't get in trouble for it, right?

Actually, I witnessed a blanket encounter once on a beach in Southern California. I had taken a walk, and since it was a rather breezy day, I had tucked myself behind a rock to get in a little reading. Engrossed in my novel, I didn't notice that company had come. I looked up to see a big brown blanket not ten yards from me. The movement of this brown mass resembled a large Mexican jumping bean.

Because of the blanket, I couldn't tell exactly what its inhabitants were doing, but with such movement and rhythm, it was unlikely that they were knitting a sweater. Granted, the beach wasn't very crowded, but we weren't the only three around. People strolled by and didn't even pay attention to this bouncing blanket. Maybe the couple just knew they wouldn't be bothered because it was Southern California.

When all movement ceased, the jumping bean peeled itself open, and out emerged a blond, bronzed, bikini-clad California couple. They picked up their blanket without a shred of guilt or concern and strolled on down the beach.

# The Law

Since there is no specific law about having sex outdoors, each case is a judgment call by the police, judge, or whatever law-enforcing body is involved. Several variables could or could not lead to an arrest for having sex outdoors:

*The discretion of the law-enforcement officer.* Believe it or not, cops wield a lot of power. They can assess a scene, and depending on their mood, degree of perversion, or religious affiliation, they can either walk away or create a big, huge, ugly scene.

*The sensitivity of the law-enforcement officer.* Some officers will be empathic and respectful of this very human act. If you have to be seen by a person of authority, it would be your good fortune to come in contact with one with such sensitivity.

Gary is one such sensible park ranger. One morning he passed a group of women hiking topless on the trail. He offered his polite ranger nod and just kept on going. (Granted, nudity isn't sex, but they often go hand in hand.)

*The state or region of the country.* This surprised me more than it probably should have. Different regions of the country and even different areas of each state have varying levels of tolerance for activities of this nature. If you are caught in Alabama, for example, you'd better hope your judge came from California. In general, the West Coast is more tolerant than the South. A California officer coming upon your intimate scene will more likely clear his or her throat and suggest that you relocate yourselves than one in Utah. There you'd better have ready either a very good alibi or influential Mormon relatives. In the Ozarks the officer may join in and tell you to keep your mouths shut and your fly open.

I heard on National Public Radio one morning that Arkansas is the only state in the union where nudity of any kind is prohibited. The governor of Arkansas hadn't taken a position to change that particular law, but he does feel people have the right to "bare arms." (We'll just call it an improper verb usage.)

***The manner in which you are conducting yourselves.*** If you are flaunting and making total pornographic spectacles of yourselves, you could either get a large sum of money from a filmmaker or you could get arrested. The possible charges include: indecent exposure, lewd conduct, or creating a public disturbance. But no law that I know of says you can get arrested for fornicating outdoors.

***The expectation of privacy.*** If you are in an area where people are expecting privacy, the judge or police may take that into account. So before you get yourselves horizontal in something other than a totally sheltered or enclosed area, take a thorough scan of your surroundings.

***The steps you take to shield yourselves from public view.*** If you are in a tent and an officer comes peering in, you are completely in the right and the officer is a voyeur.

Attorney Thomas Nast put this whole issue rather succinctly when he stated, "If you're not bothering anybody, you'll be left alone. Ninety-nine percent of the enforcement types will have a sense of humor. If you're not screwing in front of kids and are being private, you're okay."

# Safety in Numbers

No, I'm not talking about an orgy. When a police officer told me that often there is safety in numbers, he meant that having sex or being nude in a crowd of 100,000 fans at a rock concert was less likely to lead to arrest. This next story seems to put that to the test.

Back in the happy hippie days of the late 1960s, sixteen-year-old Brad was going to his first big outdoor rock concert. He planned on meeting some of his friends there. Because he had no car, he hitchhiked. What luck, the driver and his friend were going to the same concert. Brad hopped in the back and made himself comfortable. In no time at all, a big waft of smoke filled the car. "Ass, grass, or cash—nobody rides for free," said the driver as he passed Brad the biggest joint he'd ever seen. You can't be too prepared for a rock concert, you know.

Within a few hits, the car seemed to Brad to be spinning. After what seemed like minutes and hours all at the same time, they pulled into the grassy field of the concert grounds to park the car. Each of the two front-seat dwellers got out to go "water a tree" at the edge of the parking lot. Brad sat in the car for what seemed like forever. He noticed a crowd gathering at the edge of the woods. A parking lot security guy glanced over but basically ignored them. Brad went over to investigate. About twenty feet past the crowd, he saw what had caught their attention. First a bare thigh, then an arm reaching up, and an exposed breast. Then he saw a pair of bare cheeks going up and down with the rhythm of a freight train. Either that happy couple was in exhibitionist heaven, with the audience adding to their fun, or they were totally oblivious to or unconcerned about the crowd. I guess when you feel the urge—piece, baby!

# Seattle Skinny-Dippers

Occasionally there is justice. Joe and Suzie were minding their own business, discreetly skinny-dipping on a beach in Seattle. They all assumed the darkness protected them from the spying eyes of the law, and from anyone else for that matter. But then some nosy Barney Fife–type of cop thought he'd make an example of this poor pair. He not only disrupted their fun in the moonlight and generally humiliated them, but he handcuffed them and dragged their naked little bottoms down to the local police station, with full intention of throwing the book at them.

The case generated great public interest. (People love a good nudity-cop scandal.) Wonderful editorials emphasizing fig leafs and the big bad cop sprang up in almost every local publication. The couple's defense attorney, Frank Shoichet, saw it as a clear violation of their civil rights. "The couple wasn't trying to flaunt themselves in any way. Yet the officer kept their clothes as evidence. He wouldn't let them put on even a towel as he brought them into the men's booking area of the police station naked and handcuffed."

The cop's motives and past performance were immediately suspect. He in fact had a history of voyeuristic behavior and had previously gotten into trouble of this nature. (Cops run the same gamut of perversity as the general public, you know.)

Is it police brutality or some other form of police indecency to force otherwise law-abiding citizens into a public law-enforcement building without their clothes on? These two certainly thought so, and the judge agreed that the police officer was guilty of much more wrongdoing than they. The judge, Barbara Yernic (exhibiting very good judgment), dropped the charges of lewd conduct and ordered their clothes be returned. She stated that it was the most outrageously absurd thing she had ever seen. The clients settled with the police and the jail for $110,000. The cop was forced to attend a retraining program.

# Know Your Rights

If you feel you have been wrongfully treated by a law-enforcement officer, the sage advice is to calmly ride it out, write down the details, collect as much evidence as you can, and get a good attorney.

Let's take a minute to review the history of the rights of privacy that we all possess as "law-abiding Americans"—the argument used by attorney Frank Shoichet to defend the skinny-dippers.

### Ku Klux Klan Act

Back in the early 1960s, police acted in an equally unsuitable manner when they entered a black family's house, performed an illegal search, stripped the residents, and ransacked the house. The courts called this a "calculated degradation of insult and forced nakedness."

This was a direct violation of the Ku Klux Klan Act, whose intent was to combat repression visited on black people after the Civil War by the KKK and their followers in the southern white government. This act granted people the right to sue the government for "deliberate humiliation and cruelty" (as in the case of Joe and Suzie).

Originally written in 1866 and revised in 1871, it reads as follows: "Every person who, under color of any statute, ordinance, regulation, custom, or usage of any State or Territory, or the District of Columbia, subjects, or causes to be subjected, any citizen of the U.S. or other person within the jurisdiction thereof to the deprivation of any rights, privileges, or immunities secured by the Constitution and laws, shall be liable to the party injured in an action at law, suit in equity, or other proper proceeding for redress" . . . blah, blah, blah.

That's legalese for "You have the right to sue the government if they wrongfully mess with you."

Forewarned is forearmed. If you happen to be caught in a compromising position, you may be able to avoid a public scene and possible arrest if you mention cases such as that of our skinny-dippers. For all the turmoil, publicity, humiliation, and general discomfort they underwent, Joe and Suzie did receive a large sum of money. But having sex in the woods should not be considered a moneymaking proposition. (Actually, I suppose it could be quite lucrative if you were in a wealthy neighborhood and could charge the spectators!) Expecting to get wrongfully arrested in order to make money off the court system seldom seems like a worthwhile way to make a buck.

## African Peace Corps

Regional differences in sexual mores are prevalent in America, but there are also cultural differences in different parts of the world that we wouldn't think possible. E.J. served in the Peace Corps in Africa for several years. During that time she encountered some of the sexual ways and beliefs of various African tribes. In her thick Boston accent, this very spirited outdoorswoman described one bizarre sexual superstition.

According to E.J., "In Uganda's Ruwenzori Mountains [in western Uganda] women are not *allowed* into the mountains because they believe it will make them sterile. If a local man goes up the mountains with a woman, they cannot have sex while up there. The gods frown upon sex in the mountains, and local men take this very seriously. Be aware of the tribal differences: Only the Bukonjo people—the ones who live in the Ruwenzori—have these beliefs. Other tribes don't live under this rule."

## National Outdoor Intercourse Day

At Washington State University (affectionately known as WAZZU) in Pullman, Washington, having sex outside is not only a good idea, it's a holiday! The holiday slogan states, "Hooray, hooray for the eighth of May. It's National Outdoor Intercourse Day." Apparently May 8 is the equivalent of March 69, and eastern Washington is simply too damn cold in March to consider such antics. Bear in mind that this college campus is located in very rural eastern Washington, where cow tipping and watching the wheat fields grow are big sources of entertainment.

## Cyber List

While researching this chapter, I asked my lawyer what he knew about the legalities of having sex outside. A few days later I got a forwarded e-mail containing a list of weird sex laws on the books. I assumed it was from my lawyer.

Well, no one really knows who starts routing those lists of Darwin Awards, Kids Say the Darndest Things, Real Headings in Newspapers, Rules for Men, and Rules for Women—you know what I mean. Actually, this one didn't come from my attorney, it came from a guy I hadn't heard from in over a year, who had no idea I was writing a book of this nature—he just thought I'd appreciate it. Oh well, birds of a feather . . .

So here is the list I received. Like I said, I have no idea where it originated and have no way of substantiating the information without doing a ridiculous amount of work, but I thought I'd share it with you anyway. Since truth is stranger than fiction, I suspect someone really did find this stuff on the books. Besides, no one could make up rules or laws this ridiculous. But don't try to arrest anyone who may be guilty of these acts!

This list is circulating through cyberspace as "legal research" and was found in the Usenet newsgroup alt.angst. I couldn't help but add a few parenthetical comments of my own. Granted these laws aren't all about sex in the woods, but for the sake of humor, I thought you'd permit the exceptions.

### It's Against the Law

- In Alexandria, Minnesota, no man is allowed to make love to his wife with the smell of garlic, onions, or sardines on his breath. The law mandates that he must brush his teeth if his wife so requests.
- In Ames, Iowa, warn your hubby that after lovemaking, he isn't allowed to take more than three gulps of beer while lying in bed with you or while holding you in his arms.
- Bozeman, Montana, has a law that bans all sexual activity between nude members of the opposite sex in the front yard of a home after sundown. (Apparently, if you're gay or wearing socks, you're safe from the law!) (Is that considered safe socks?)
- During lunch breaks in Carlsbad, New Mexico, no couple may engage in a sexual act while parked in their vehicle, unless their car has curtains.
- Clinton, Oklahoma, has a law against masturbating while watching two people having sex in a car.
- It's safe to make love while parked in Coeur d'Alene, Idaho. Police officers aren't allowed to

walk up and knock on the window. Any suspicious officer who thinks that sex is taking place must drive up from behind, honk his horn three times, and wait approximately two minutes before getting out of his car to investigate. (Okay, there's a law that makes sense.)

- In Connorsville, Wisconsin, no man may shoot off a gun while his female partner is having an orgasm.

- In Detroit couples are not allowed to make love in an automobile unless the act takes place while the vehicle is parked on the couple's own property.

- A law in Fairbanks, Alaska, does not allow moose to have sex on city streets. (But who's going to stop them?)

- In Harrisburg, Pennsylvania, it is illegal to have sex with a truck driver inside a tollbooth.

- Every hotel in Hastings, Nebraska, is required to provide each guest with a clean and pressed nightshirt. No couple, even if they are married, may sleep together in the nude. Nor may they have sex unless they are wearing one of these clean, white cotton nightshirts. (Could this be the result of a lobbying effort from the nightshirt company?)

- A law in Helena, Montana, mandates that a woman can't dance on a table in a saloon or bar unless she has on at least three pounds and two ounces of clothing. (That would be one heavy G-string!)

- A state law in Illinois mandates that all bachelors should be called master, not mister, when addressed by their female counterparts. (Oh, please!)

- An excerpt from a brilliant piece of Kentucky state legislation: "No female shall appear in a bathing suit on any highway within this state unless she be escorted by at least two officers or unless she be armed with a club."

- But note the following important amendment: "The provisions of this statute shall not apply to females weighing less than 90 pounds nor exceeding 200 pounds, nor shall it apply to male horses."

- In Kingsville, Texas, there is a law against two pigs having sex on the city's airport property.

- Any couple making out inside a vehicle and accidentally sounding the horn during their lustful act may be taken to jail, according to a Liberty Corner, New Jersey, law. (A good reason to have sex in the backseat.)

- In Los Angeles a man is legally entitled to beat his wife with a leather belt or strap, but the belt can't be wider than two inches unless he has his wife's consent to beat her with a wider strap. Consent should be given prior to the event. (I'm surprised O.J. didn't try to use this in his defense.)

- In Merryville, Missouri, women are prohibited from wearing corsets because "the privilege of admiring the curvaceous, unencumbered body of a young woman should not be denied to the normal, red-blooded American male."

- In Norfolk, Virginia, a woman can't go out without wearing a corset. There was a civil service job—for men only—called a corset inspector.

- In Michigan a woman isn't allowed to cut her own hair without her husband's permission.

- In Nevada sex without a condom is illegal. (In other states it's just lethal.)

- An ordinance in Newcastle, Wyoming, specifically bans couples from having sex while standing inside a store's walk-in meat freezer!

- In Oblong, Illinois, it's punishable by law to make love while hunting or fishing on your wedding day.
- In Oxford, Ohio, it's illegal for a woman to strip off her clothing while standing in front of a man's picture.
- In hotels in Sioux Falls, South Dakota, every room is required to have twin beds. And when a couple rents a room for only one night, the beds must always be a minimum of two feet apart. And it's illegal to make love on the floor between the beds!
- A Tremonton, Utah, law states that no woman may have sex with a man while riding in an ambulance. In addition to normal charges, the woman's name will be published in the local newspaper. The man does not receive any punishment.
- Utah state legislation outlaws all sex with anyone but your spouse. In addition, adultery, oral and anal sex, and masturbation are considered sodomy and can lead to imprisonment. But sex with an animal—unless performed for profit— is *not* considered sodomy. Polygamy—provided only the missionary position is applied—is only a misdemeanor.
- In Ventura County, California, cats and dogs are not allowed to have sex without a permit.
- The only legal sexual position in Washington, D.C., is the missionary position.
- In Willowdale, Oregon, no man may curse while having sex with his wife.
- The state of Washington bars having sex with a virgin under any circumstances.
- In Florida it is illegal for a single, divorced, or widowed woman to parachute on Sunday afternoons.

Strange laws have been on the books since way before cyber-days. You've got to wonder why some of these laws were even conceived. The following are from *Facts and Phalluses* by Alexandra Parsons:

*"Any knight under the rank of a lord or any other person [is forbidden to wear] any gowne, jaket, or cloke unless it be of sufficient length on a man standing upright to cover his privy member and buttokkes."*

—LAW PASSED IN 1548 BY KING EDWARD VI

In English law, indecent exposure, which is defined as the display of the penis, flaccid or erect, toward a person of the opposite sex, is an exclusively male offense. It is the most common sexual misdemeanor.

## In Conclusion

As far as having sex in the woods goes, it feels great and it's not illegal. What more could you ask for? Of course, use your discretion and remember that you have rights. Even if you don't know the specific laws, you can probably guess based on the general moral attitude of the region. No matter where you are, it is highly recommended to simply *cover your ass*.

# Chapter 11

## THAT WAS THEN, THIS IS NOW

*"At some point in your life you'd rather be caught by your parents than your kids."*

—TOM WILMOT

**T**he previous chapters have focused mainly on younger campers and, in particular, on the young "in love" couple camping together for the first time. You know the stage, when everything is still cute; when you're willing to stay up till dawn making love, then get up three hours later and hike all day; when you would forfeit your gear for your lover's comfort, and break wood with your bare hands to impress her. Ah, those were the days, my friend.

This is now. Times have changed since some of those first camping experiences. Back when you were twenty, the ground seemed softer, the crickets were quieter, the sleeping bag had more room, and there were no bored and bickering kids requiring your constant attention. Now you can't just grab your partner and go for the gusto. Life is much more complicated.

# Plowing the Back Forty

Rick and his lovely wife Robin live on eight wooded acres. Rick thought it would be fun to rekindle with her some of their younger romantic days of frolicking in their woods. "Come on, honey," he said one day. "Let's go plow the back forty like we used to." She was somewhat reticent, as visions of the kids, the neighbors, and the uncomfortable ground all came flooding into her mind. Rick gave her the convincing argument that they lived on eight very rural acres in the hills of Vermont, and virtually no one ever went back there. Unable to refuse his puppy-dog look, she conceded.

No sooner had they gotten themselves all situated and disrobed when they heard voices. They both froze and shushed each other until they practically burst out laughing. The neighbors from next door were out cutting through the back woods, heading toward God knew where! All Robin could think of was the PTA, a town scandal, and the kids. After the threat of being caught had passed, they both lay there laughing in relieved hysteria. "I'm too old for this," Robin claimed.

As she relayed this story to me, Robin said, "As grown-ups, you have sex in a bed because you *have* a bed and because you're *allowed* to have sex in a bed."

# Camping Queries

In the summer of your life, when it's been years since you've had a romantic weekend in the woods, planning for such a venture will trigger lots of questions that never seemed to arise before:

*Did your spouse pack appropriately?* When packing for a later-in-life camping trip, double-check your spouse's pack. I mean, you don't want to be outside without the poncho. In your youth sleeping bag activity would have kept you warm through a rainstorm, raincoat or no raincoat. Now you're more interested in staying warm and dry and getting a good night's sleep.

***If you had to forget one thing, would it be the birth-control device or the coffee?*** In your younger years you wouldn't have thought twice about that one. But now going without your morning coffee would not be a pretty sight.

***Is now really the time to grow that beard?*** "I thought you wanted a romantic week with me?" Alice asked Tim. "Why did you stop shaving the first day out?" When going on a camping trip, men often leave the razor home. They equate being out in the woods with the burly "back to nature" feel and let the beard go. Well, stubbles may feel good to you, but they can be hell on your poor wife's face (and thighs).

***Will she still be interested in me?*** Guess what—ten years later, foreplay still counts. There may not still be the same excitement, but foreplay and romance are still important— maybe more important now than in your groping, ever-ready, inexperienced youth.

Take advantage of your increased maturity and the relaxation that can come from familiarity. But also take advantage of the opportunity to experiment with new ways of being together. Novelty and a fresh approach may rekindle some old embers.

***Will this old camping equipment do?*** If you haven't used that tent and those sleeping bags within the past fifteen years, at the very least inspect them well before you leave. Equipment today is so much more comfortable and design is so much better. Splurge on yourselves.

***What about the sleep pads?*** When you were younger, more starry-eyed, and hornier, many things were tolerable. Actually, you didn't even notice them. Sleeping on a rock-studded ground was fine. Now invest in a more expensive Therm-a-Rest pad. Go for the deluxe model. It's longer, wider, and thicker—and so (probably) are you.

# Camping with Kids

Older married campers ask a common question: Can you have a romantic weekend in the woods with your spouse—with the kids? What's one free hour of indulgence really worth? If, after you're all finished and rosy, you have to get a forest ranger to help you find the kids, was it worth it?

Money can't necessarily buy love, but it can certainly buy entertainment and distraction for the kids. Many kinds of group and family outdoor programs include childcare experts to educate and, more important, entertain your kids. Some groups have naturalists, athletes, craftspeople, and general-kid-care kind of people.

## Tips for Hiking Trips with Kids

- Before the trip have a trail-mix-makin' party. Poll the kids for their favorite nuts, cereal, and dried fruit. Pile all the ingredients onto the table, have the kids "permanent marker" their own Ziploc Baggies, and fill them with the snacks of their choice.

- Buy a bunch of disposable water bottles, and color-code them with string or yarn tied on each bottle. Choose a different color for each person.

- Powdered Gatorade will keep the kids hydrated. They're more likely to drink water that's flavored.

- If you will be hiking with guides who provide meals, get their menu ahead of time. That way you can bring alternative food to accommodate picky eaters.

- Bring cash or travelers' checks. Wilderness emergencies seldom are resolved with credit cards.

- Inquire about the length and difficulty of a hike before you establish an itinerary. Two of the five kids of some Grand Canyon prehoneymooners couldn't handle the hike out. They had to be helicoptered out at fifty-five dollars each. In a state of newly engaged bliss, this fiasco was no big deal. I wonder what happened when they became a *five*-teenager household!

# Maine Guides

In the 1940s and 1950s, it was common and economically feasible for a family to pack up the kids and rent a cabin for a week or two up in the hills of Maine, Minnesota, or lots of other places with beautiful outdoors. You may think people were more puritanical back in the 1940s and 1950s. Granted, they may have touted a more "holier than thou" line than we often hear today, but do you, for a minute, think those folks wanted to baby-sit their own kids the whole time during their two weeks of togetherness? Do you think they sacrificed their privacy for the sake of the children? *No!*

They hired a guide—a college student or high school kid who rented herself out to cook, clean, and above all keep the kids from killing each other or themselves. Guides worked for slave wages of one to five dollars a day. At the end of a few weeks, that money looked like a big deal. And it was—compared with taking care of a bunch of younger siblings for no money whatsoever.

There also was the much more expensive solution of an au pair or nanny who accompanies the family on all their outings. Remember *The Brady Bunch*'s Alice?

Those hired caretakers aren't completely a thing of the past, but today they sure cost a lot more than a few bucks a week. Nowadays, privacy in the woods is going to cost you— big-time.

Also, today's parents often have so little time with their

children that they relish togetherness while on vacation. But couples have less time together, too. So how can we get both—kid time and intimate time?

## Love Tips with Camper Kids

Parents have been outsmarting their kids ever since kids began. Here are a few helpful suggestions from seasoned family campers:

- If you want real family coziness for the whole trip, bring one tent. Tent manufacturers helped make this possible with two-room family tents. Eureka makes a 10.5-by-20-foot Condo Family Tent with two rooms and lots of ventilation. Wenzel also makes a less expensive two-room family dome. Still it's not like two layers of ripstop nylon are going to eliminate the sounds of two slippery sleeping bags swishing together.
- If you have any hope of getting some real private time with your spouse, bring two tents—and set them up a little distance away from each other.
- Bring a sheet to help muffle the sounds of sleeping bags in motion. A transistor radio will also camouflage the sounds of two intimate bodies.
- No candles or flashlights should be allowed in the tent. Light on the inside casts detailed shadows on the outside. With kids outside or in the neighboring tent, this is no time for "enlightenment."
- Another trick is to physically exhaust your kids without exhausting yourselves. You'll both want to have at least a little bit of fuel left to stoke the fires of passion.

# Love-Life Savings Time

Sometimes your wristwatch may hold the key to privacy. Although Cindy is not really a control freak, she has mastered the art of controlling time. (What power!) "As soon as we're beyond all threat of seeing a clock with the real time, I set everyone's watches ahead an hour. The watch says nine P.M.; it's really eight P.M.—it's bedtime. Good night." So what if the sun is still high in the sky? "Kids, pretend you're in Alaska—land of the midnight sun." Hey, if we manipulate time for daylight savings time, why not? It's "love-life savings time."

# Skinny-Dipping with the Kids

Should parents still skinny-dip when kids start wearing suits? Until early adolescence, kids will skinny-dip along with the parents and think nothing of it. Once kids reach puberty, however, two things are bound to happen. First: Modesty sets in—in a big way. Adolescents become very self-conscious about their bodies, and nobody is going to view them unclothed.

Second: *Everything* you do will embarrass your kid. "Mom, how could you do that? You're embarrassing me!" is not a question or even a statement. It becomes a mantra, repeated several times a day no matter what you do to avoid it. You can embarrass your kids even if no one else is there.

Can you respect your kids' desire to not see you, or be seen by you, naked? It is a philosophical question that you and your spouse need to ponder. Perhaps now that they are old enough to have such opinions, they are also old enough to be on their own for a while, and you can bare your buns to the sun goddesses in peace. Which brings up the other question: If you finally have a little bit of private time, would you rather spend it naked in the water or naked in the tent?

# Have No Fear, Bare Your Rear!

Given a little effort, problems can soon become "creative solutions." If you are a family who really enjoys nudity and feel as comfortable with your clothes off as on, perhaps you want to join the club—the American Association for Nude Recreation (AANR), that is. You're not the last 1960s survivors to appreciate that free feeling of bouncing, flopping, and jiggling in the breeze. Turn on—tune in—take it off! Connect with people who have remained uninhibited into the twenty-first century. With 50,000 members strong, a lot of bare butts are hanging out.

For those of you who enjoy nudity without the gawking or flirting, there are several nudist communities around the country. (The term nudist *colony* went out with poodle skirts.) One chapter of the AANR was featured in an article in *The Boston Globe*. Solair Recreation League, a nudist resort in Woodstock, Connecticut, has been open since 1937 and currently has 300 full-time members (who are willing to pay the $1,333.50 per-couple annual fee). On 350 beautifully wooded acres, people swim, play tennis, golf, hike, and do everything else that clothed people do to relax and recreate. Butt they do it naked!

When I visited the resort, I didn't get the impression it was a *Baywatch* babe scene. Solair has the same five percent of "body beautifuls" that are walking the streets. (This five percent become fashion models and demonstrate a look the rest of us can only hope to achieve.)

Would teenagers be interested? If they have been hanging out their whole lives in a place where nudity is the norm, then it's not a taboo for them. The article spoke of teenage girls nonchalantly strolling past middle-aged men. "I'm naked," one of them said, shrugging. "So, what's the big deal?"

For the record, Solair Recreation League screens its

members thoroughly to weed out those who are there only to gawk.

## Cybersex in the Woods

This book would not be complete if I didn't bring sex in the woods into the computer age. I went online for some of my research, and I also thought a chat room could provide me with some interesting material.

For those of you new to chat rooms, beware! I figured it would be a good place to get stories of people's outdoor intimate adventures. Being a chat-room virgin, if you will, I was a little nervous. I hesitated for days.

Finally, I logged onto the "Great Outdoors" chat feature section and posed my question: "I'm doing research on comical outdoor 'intimate' experiences. Do you have any that you could tell me?" I assumed this would be clear enough.

In a chat room, it turns out, you are at the mercy of the "luck of the draw" and can talk only to whoever happens to be logged on at the same time. You never know who will just happen to be there.

The regulars—those logged on at work, paid to be at their desks—stay tuned in all day. They have their computers set to several different chat rooms and check in each time they hear the little chat-room *ding*.

The suburban housewives are either (understandably) looking for conversation with more than four-word sentences, or are seeking information about which disposable diaper absorbs the most.

And the kids—you have to be careful about kids. Although one is supposed to be eighteen to enter, it's hard to ask for ID on a computer, and every underage kid, upon being asked, would (of course) give out the correct age. I figured that my inquiry about "comical outdoor 'intimate' experiences" was couched in enough rhetoric that a kid wouldn't recognize that I was asking about sex. What kids, regardless of what they know about it, refer to sex as an " 'intimate' experience"?

## Chat-Room Chat

These were my actual encounters. Maybe I need more practice to get the hang of it!

**Lu:** I'm doing research on comical outdoor "intimate" experiences.

### Instant Message 1

**DD:** Are you feeling frisky?
**Lu:** *(Oh great! This is just what I was afraid of!)* No, not really, I just need stories about some of the funny personal things that happen to people out in the woods.
   *(No response—good!)*

### Instant Message 2

**JB333:** Like falling out a tree butt naked?
**Lu:** Yeah, but what happened?
**JB333:** We just got off balance somehow. She screamed, guess I did, too, before we hit the ground. *(I told him about the hammock for two, should he find himself feeling like George of the Jungle again.)*

### Instant Message 3

**MM2:** I've done it in every park in New Jersey.
**Lu:** *(finding that bizarre, but not particularly interesting or comical)* Can you give me more details?
**MM2:** Call me and I'll tell you all about it.
**Lu:** *(That wasn't an option. I was already beginning to feel creepy,*

*but didn't want to lose the story.)* Type in your story. Did anything funny or exciting happen?

**MM2:**  Got caught by police, park rangers, people camping, and lifeguards.

**Lu:**  *(I'm feeling even creepier. Obviously this guy has no discretionary skills.)* What did you do? Who were you with? Did you get arrested?

**MM2**:  Call me and I'll tell you all about it.

**Lu:**  *(Okay, even I know when to surrender—no details were coming my way without a phone call, and there's no way in hell I was calling that jerk!)*

Chat over! Disconnect!

# CONCLUSION

Congratulations! You can now consider yourself the sex-in-the-woods expert in your neighborhood. You are equipped with knowledge of the latest and the greatest in equipment, contraception, and techniques, for safe and environmentally friendly outdoor loving. You've even broadened your repertoire of sex games and improved your cooking techniques. Not bad for one book.

We live in such a high-tech world that even something as basic as making love requires a larger degree of equipment, rules, and preparation than before. You have just witnessed the joys and perils of taking a natural act and putting it into its natural setting, where it originally began. If, while reading this book, you are in some way inspired to commune with nature, I consider this a success.

The stories you have just read are true, but obviously most of the names (and a few details) have been changed to protect the libidinous. If any of these stories sounds like yours, it may be. If one sounds like fun, go make it happen, and have a great time!

# Resources

## Outdoor Recreation Groups

**American Association for Nude Recreation**
Solair Recreation League
Woodstock, CT
Nudist community
$1,333.50 a season (per couple)

**Appalachian Mountain Club**
5 Joy Street
Boston, MA 02108
(617) 523-0636
www.outdoors.org

**The Mountaineers Club**
300 Avenue West
Seattle, WA 98119
(800) 573-8484
(800) 284-8554
www.mountaineers.org

**National Forest Service**
Fire regulations, updated trail information, etc.
www.fs.fed.us

**National Outdoor Leadership School (NOLS)**
288 Main Street
Lander, WY 82520-3140

(307) 332-5300
www.nols.edu

**New England Forest Service**
(603) 528-8721
www.fs.fed.us/r9/white

**Potomac Appalachian Trail Club (PATC)**
118 Park Street, S.E.
Vienna, VA 22180
(703) 242-0693
www.PATC.net
(Call Mon.–Thurs. 7 P.M. to 9 P.M., or Thurs.–Fri. noon to 2 P.M.)
*Information guide to PATC cabins:* available for $4 ($3.20 for members)
*To rent a cabin:* Call at the above hours only, or write.

**U.S. Forest Service**
www.fs.fed.us

## Outdoor Recreation Gear and Apparel

### Suppliers

**Brookstone, Inc.**
17 Riverside Street
Nashua, NH 03062
(603) 880-9500
www.brookstoneonline.com
(online store)

**Campmor**
28 Parkway
P.O. Box 700-M
Saddle River, NJ 07458-0700
(800) CAMPMOR
www.campmor.com (online store)

**Cascade Designs, Inc.**
4000 First Avenue South
Seattle, WA 98134
(800) 531-9531
www.cascadedesigns.com
consumer@cascadedesigns.com

**GO! Activewear Outlet**
121 Madison Avenue
West Yellowstone, MT 59758
(406) 646-4850

**LL Bean**
Freeport, ME 04033
(800) 221-4221
www.llbean.com

**MooseJaw Online Catalog**
www.moosejawonline.com

**New Tribe**
Tom Ness and Sophia Sparks
5517 Riverbanks Road
Grants Pass, OR 97527
(541) 476-9492
newtribe@cdsnet.net

**Outdoor Research (OR)**
www.orgear.com
Outfitters and Reviews
The Gear Addict
www.web-dzine.com/gearaddict/reviews

**Recreational Equipment Incorporated (REI)**
1700 45th Street, East
Sumner, WA 98352
(800) 426-4840
www.rei.com (online store)

**Title Nine Sports**
5743 Landregan Street
Emeryville, CA 94608
(800) 609-0092
www.thefolks@title9sports.com

**TravelSmith**
P.O. Box 5729
Novato, CA 94948
(800) 950-1600
www.travelsmith.com

**Zanika Sportswear**
(612) 529-1785; (612) 521-4481
(fax)
www.ool.com/zanika.html

## Sleeping Bags and Pads

**Caribou Mountaineering Joint Venture**
400 Commerce Road
Alice, TX 78332
(800)824-4153; (512)668-3769
(fax)
www.caribou.com
price: $86

**Cascade Designs Staytek Double Wide Therm-a-Rest (inflatable pad)**
price: $180
available from REI

**Cascade Designs Therm-a-Coupl'R 25**
price: $70
available from REI

**Outdoor Research Double Bivy Sack**
Outdoor Research Advanced Double Bivy Sack
price: $390
available from REI
www.orgear.com

## Tents

**Eureka**
Condo Family Tent
price: $900
Two-Room Family Lodge
price: $400
available from Campor, REI

**Wenzel**
Two-Room Family Dome
price: $140
available from Campor

## Hammocks

**Cozy (insulator)**
price: $40
available from New Tribe

**Reversible Sunbrella Hammock Pad**
price: $100
available from Brookstone

**Reversible Sunbrella Pillow**
price: $40
available from Brookstone

**Treeboat**
price: $80
available from New Tribe

## Women's Outdoor Garments and Undergarments

### Moving Comfort undergarments (made with QuickWick)
including Quick Dry Travel Briefs
price: $13
available from GO! Activewear Outlet, REI, and other sport outlets

### Title Nine Sports Struggle-Free, Zip-Front Bra
5743 Landregan Street
Emeryville, CA 94608
(800) 609-0092
www.thefolks@title9sports.com
price: $35

### Wild Roses
www.orgear.com
Wild Roses will be available at finer outdoor specialty shops nationwide in Fall 1999.

### Women's Outdoor Clothing System
available from Zanika Sportswear

### Camping Necessities

#### *Lanterns and Binoculars*

### Night Quest Binoculars (REI)
See at night without a flashlight, $1,745–$2,245.

### REI Mini Candle Lantern
price: $10
aluminum lantern: $15
brass lantern: $25
available from REI
Eveready makes three versions of 2-in-1 Area Lights. Slide back the battery and they change from flashlights to lanterns. Bright krypton bulb. Batteries from REI.

1. Lantern/Sport Area Lantern, 6V lantern battery, 2 lbs. 6 oz., $17
2. Powered by 4AA batteries, 5″×3″ closed, 8 oz., $10
3. Compact 2-in-1 Light, 2 AA batteries, 5.5 oz., $9

#### *Organizers*

### Outdoor Research Outdoor Organizer
price: $18
available from REI

### Outdoor Research Travel Kits
Compact Travel Kit: $22.99
Standard Travel Kit: $34.99
available from Campmor, REI

### Outdoor Research Woman's Trail Kit (includes condoms)
price: $20

**Outdoor Research Woman's Travel Kit**
price: $39.99
available from Campmor, REI

*Accessories*

**Outdoor Blanket by Design Salt**
price: $69
available from REI, Design Salt
(800) 254-7258

**Wool Picnic Throw**
price: $62
available from L.L. Bean

*Cleaning Gear*

**Cascade Designs PackTowl**
sizes: from 10″×27″ to 39″×59″
prices: from $6 to $20
available from REI, Campmor

**Crystal Stick Body Deodorant**
F/T Ltd.
P.O. Box 756
Millbrae, CA 94030
Product of Thailand
prices: $2.00 travel size, $8.50 for the large one in the push-up container

**SunShower by Basic Designs**
Sunshower II: $12.99
Sunshower III: $19.99

Sunshower IV: $30
shower enclosure: $24
available from REI, Campmor

**Travel Suds, Sierra Dawn Products**
Sebastopol, CA 95472
price: $2.75/2-ounce refill
available from REI

*Other*

**BayGen Power Group**
80 Amity Road
Warwick, NY 10990
Freeplay Self-Powered Radios
price: $80
(800) WIND234
www.freeplay.net
available from Sharper Image, Brookstone

**Garrity Flashlight**
price: from $8 to $12
available from REI and hardware stores

**Self-Powered AM/FM Radio**
price: $200
available from C. Crane Company
1001 Main Street
Fortuna, CA 95540
(800) 522-8863
www.ccrane.com

## Insect Deterrents

### Blocker
Verdant Brands, Inc.
9555 James Avenue South
Suite 200
Bloomington, MN 55431
price: $8 to $10 for 4-ounce
lotion
available from Solutions Catalog,
(800) 342-9988, CVS, True
Value, REI

### Duranon Tick Repellant
Coulston
P.O. Box 30
Easton, PA 18044-0030
(215) 253-0167

### HourGuard
By Amway
(800) 544-7167
price: $12/tube
Product information: 25%
DEET

### Mississauga Mosquito Jacket
price: $15
matching pants: $9
available from 3164 Peppermill
Ct., Mississauga, Ontario,
Canada L5L 4X4L
905-820-7000

### Sawyer Products
P.O. Box 188
Safety Harbor, FL 34695
(800) 940-4464
Controlled Release DEET
formula (20%)
2-ounce lotion: $5
4-ounce lotion: $6
Encapsulates DEET in skin-
friendly protein.
Eco Pump

### Skedaddle 4-Hour Insect Protection
(800) 243-2929

### Tec-Labs Clearly Cala Anti-Itch Medicated Gel
Tec Laboratories
P.O. Box 1958
Albany, OR 97321
(800) ITCHING
www.teclabsinc.com

### Travel Medicine

### SCS International
(800) 749-8425
www.1800PIXTICK.com

(800) 872-8633
www.travmed.com

### Traveller's Mosquito Net
price: $39.99
available from Campmor

# Sex Products and Paraphernalia

## Suppliers

### Emergency Contraception
Preven (emergency
contraception kit)
price: about $20
distributed by Gynetics, Inc., NJ
See your doctor or pharmacist.

### Executive Affairs
(800) 615-4188
www.executiveaffairs.com

### A Nice Place to Buy Lingerie
www.cyberhomeshow.com/
lingerie/lin1.htm

### Sex Mall's Sextoy Warehouse
webcreator.mainquad.com/
users/x777/sextoy8.htm

### Voyages
VCG
P.O. Box 78550
San Francisco, CA 94107-8550
www.voyages.com

### Wicked Temptations
(800) 883-9693
www.wickedtemptations.com

## Oils and Lotions

### AstroGlide
BioFilm, Inc.
Vista, CA 92083
Foille Ointment (for minor
burns and sunburn)
Carbisulphoil Company
Dallas, TX 75204
www.astroglide.com

### Lush Massage Bar
P.O. Box 71029
Vancouver, BC V6P 3T1
(888) 733-5874
www.LushCanada.com
price: $5.95

### Myo-Ther Massage Lotion
Parodel Products
1379 Colborne Street
East Brantford, Ontario N3T 5M1
(888) 727-2335
prices: $16.95 (32 oz.), $39.95
(28 oz.)

### Vaginal Contraceptive Film
(VCF)
Made by Apothecus
Pharmaceutical Corp.
(800) 879-2393
prices: $4 (for 3),
$11 (for 12)
available at most pharmacies

**Harness**

**Ness Saddle**
price: $70
available from New Tribe

**Sex for One**

**Aqua Vulva**
Aqua Vulva
P.O. Box 8070
Madeira Beach, FL 33738-8070
(800) 292-9173
www.aquavulva.com

# Books

## Cabins and Lookouts

Foley, Tom, and Tish Steinfeld,
*How to Rent a Fire Lookout in the
Pacific Northwest: A Guide to
Renting Fire Lookouts, Guard
Stations, Ranger Cabins, Warming
Shelters, and Bunkhouses*
(Wilderness Press, 1996), $12.95
Gatesy, Carolyne Ilona,
*Firetowers, Lookouts, and Rustic
Cabins for Rent* (Bear Mountain
Press, 1997), $14.95

## Camp Cookbooks

Jacobson, Cliff, *Basic Essentials of
Cooking in the Outdoors* (ICS
Books, 1989), $5.99

NOLS Staff, *NOLS Cookery,* 4th
ed. (Stackpole Books, 1997),
$12.95
Siegel, Helene, and Karen
Gillingham, *Totally Camping
Cookbook* (Ten Speed Press,
1996), $4.95

## Other

Bezruchka, Stephen, M.D., *The
Pocket Doctor* (The Mountaineers,
1992), $4.95
Dorling, Ann Hooper, *The
Ultimate Sex Book* (Kindersley,
1992), $29.95
Gorman, Stephen, *AMC Guide to
Winter Camping* (Appalachian
Mountain Club Books, 1991),
$12.95
Love, Jesse W., *Everyone's Guide to
Hot Springs of Western Washington*
(Kaleidoscope Publications Inc.,
1985)
Marsh, Carol, and Arthur
Upgren, *Asteroids, Comets, and
Meteors (Secrets of Space)* (School &
Library Binding, 1996), $20.40
Newman, Bob, *Common Sense
Survival for Outdoor Enthusiasts*
(Menasha Ridge Press, 1994),
$4.95
Seaborg, Eric, and Ellen Dudley,
*Hiking and Backpacking* (Human
Kinetics Publishers, Inc., 1994),
$12.95

Viehman, John, *Trailside's Hints and Tips for Outdoor Adventure* (Rodale Press, 1993), $9.95

**Bookstores**

**Adventurous Traveler Bookstore**
245 South Champlain
Burlington, VT 05401
(800) 282-3963

www.adventuroustraveler.com/
www.gorp.com/atbook.htm

**Mountaineers Bookstore**
The Mountaineers Club
300 Third Avenue West
Seattle, WA 98119
(800) 284-8554
www.mountaineers.org

# About the Author

LUANN COLOMBO, an avid outdoor enthusiast, received her master's in science education at Western Washington University, where she completed a wilderness education block of courses. She has written more than thirty books and CD-ROMS for kids on science and nature, and she lectures on sex-related topics through Planned Parenthood and the American Cancer Society. She is an active member of the Association of Sex Educators and Trainers (ASSET) and lives with her husband in Littleton, Massachusetts.